How to Remain Ever free

Publishers
Pustak Mahal®, Delhi

J-3/16 , Daryaganj, New Delhi-110002
☎ 23276539, 23272783, 23272784 • *Fax:* 011-23260518
E-mail: info@pustakmahal.com • *Website:* www.pustakmahal.com

Sales Centres
10-B, Netaji Subhash Marg, Daryaganj, New Delhi-110002
☎ 23268292, 23268293, 23279900 • *Fax:* 011-23280567
E-mail: rapidexdelhi@indiatimes.com

Branch Offices
Bangalore: ☎ 22234025
E-mail: pmblr@sancharnet.in • pustak@sancharnet.in
Mumbai: ☎ 22010941
E-mail: rapidex@bom5.vsnl.net.in
Patna: ☎ 3094193 • *Telefax:* 0612-2302719
E-mail: rapidexptn@rediffmail.com
Hyderabad: *Telefax:* 040-24737290
E-mail: pustakmahalhyd@yahoo.co.in

© **Author**

ISBN 81-223-0929-1

Edition : January 2006

Printed at : Param Offsetters, Okhla, New Delhi-110020

Preface

Way back in 1994, I had written my first book titled, *How to Remain Ever Happy*. I got an overwhelming response from the readers about this book much beyond my expectation and I am still receiving a steady stream of letters and phone calls from various readers. While writing the book, I never imagined that God will shower so much grace on the book.

Many of the readers were so much fascinated by that book that they had been regularly asking me to write some more books on similar pattern, because they said that the content and the style of the book is very reader friendly and thought provoking. I hope their prayers have been answered in the form of the present book in their hands.

Like the previous book, this book also started out of a sudden inspiration from God and my pen began writing effortlessly as if ideas were pouring into my mind from some inexhaustible source, and my pen stopped only at the virtual completion of the book.

This book contains many gems of wisdom which have been tried and tested by innumerable persons in the past who have treaded the path to liberation and happiness. I hope that this book will prove equally useful and interesting as my earlier book, *How to Remain Ever Happy* and will work as a companion guide to that book. While reading the book, you may find some points corelated in various chapters of the book and also with my earlier written books which is inevitable in such type of works and this will only help you to reinforce these points more strongly in your mind rather than giving a feeling of repetition.

I wish that the readers will extract the fullest advantage of every bit of the knowledge contained in the foregoing pages of this book.

M. K. Gupta
Nuclear Science Centre (JNU campus),
Aruna Asaf Ali Marg, Near Vasant Kunj,
New Delhi-110 067.
Tel: 26892601, 26892603, 9891988230.
Email: *mkg@nsc.ernet.in.*

Contents

What is Real Freedom?

Freedom is intrinsic to happiness. Unless you feel free inside, you can't be happy. A person who is a slave and is in bondage remains always miserable and can never experience the inner happiness. But first, we have to understand as to what is real freedom. Normally, people think that freedom means that you should be able to do whatever you like without any restriction. For example, a corrupt person may think that if he may be given complete freedom, he will take as much bribe as possible and will amass as much wealth as possible. A criminal may think of doing various crimes freely if he is not restricted by law and police. A sex maniac may think of indulging in as much sex as possible if left free.

But this is not true freedom. A person running madly after money is not a free person. Rather, he is a slave to money. Such a person is very much dependent and attached to money and can't live without it. Can you call such a person 'free'? He is greatly imprisoned and tied by the chains of money. **An attached person is never a free person. In fact, he is a slave.**

Real freedom or rather spiritual freedom is not the freedom to do anything you feel like. Real freedom is a state of mind where you do not feel bound and imprisoned by anything in life. You may deal with a thing, enjoy a thing but you don't become emotionally entangled and remain tied to it for long. In spiritual parlance, you remain detached. **In this state, you continuously die to the past and keep yourself in the present,** i.e., you involve yourself in a particular thing with full attention and awareness, perform it as best as you can, enjoy it to the fullest and then let it go completely after the activity is over, bringing your attention to the next thing in hand.

You can also say that in real freedom you remain a 'Master' while dealing and enjoying a thing. You do not become dependent and a slave to anything or any pleasure. You become bigger than all things and pleasures. When you want to enjoy a thing, you can, but when you don't want to enjoy it, it can't disturb your peace.

It is to be noted that real freedom is the freedom only from what is false, useless and unreal and not freedom from what is useful, beneficial and real. The only thing is that you have to deal with the useful in a detached manner like a Master. Real freedom is not leaving your family, money or possessions or throwing everything and going to a faraway place, living totally alone. It is more of a change in your mental attitude rather than physical separation. **So real freedom is not the freedom of ego to do anything one likes but it is the freedom from ego and Lower nature and to emerge in your Higher nature, where you act like a 'Master'.** While functioning under the Lower nature, you feel like a slave being pulled by some unconscious force having no control on yourself. On the other hand, under Higher nature, you are fully conscious and in absolute control like a 'Master'.

Many people also have a misunderstanding about the word, 'detachment'. They think that 'detachment' means total indifference to what you are seeing and doing. This is incorrect. **Detachment is not a dead and dull response to a thing. On the other hand, detachment implies to a fully alive and sensitive response in the present moment** which is associated with full attention, awareness, mindfulness and full sensory and emotional joy the moment contains, but restricted only to the present moment. As soon as the moment is over, you let go of the past event and become wide awake and fresh for the next moment. You don't linger in the past. **So detachment is not becoming dead to the present but becoming dead to the past**. Of course, you will definitely remain indifferent/dead towards the thing you are not dealing or concerned with in the present.

It is also to be noted that real freedom consists of not only keeping yourself free but also respecting the freedom of others, i.e., your freedom should not intrude into the freedom of others. You should also allow others to be free and independent and have their own space and should not force them to change, not impose your view point on them and not interfere in their activities. In your hand lies the responsibility of your own development and not forcing others to change. You can't mend or change a person against his own desire. Of course, if someone wants help and advice from you in changing himself or herself, you should gladly offer.

It should also be borne in mind that restrictions imposed by the law and society on your conduct and behaviour have nothing to do with the real inner or spiritual freedom, we are talking about. These restrictions, rules, regulations and punishments are simply designed to maintain the outward law and harmony in the society or state by reducing conflicts, quarrels, riots, crimes, terrorism, etc. These restrictions have nothing to do with the inner spiritual freedom and shouldn't be taken as a curtailment of our real freedom. Similarly, when an organisation makes some rules and regulations to discipline its employees and punish the erring employees, it shouldn't be construed as a violation of your inner freedom. This is only to run the system in an efficient and organised manner.

Now to reach to this state of real freedom or rather real detachment, two things are needed:

1. Correct knowledge/understanding/wisdom about the truths and facts of life or in short, the knowledge of reality.

2. Applying will power and control in your day-to-day life based on this correct knowledge and understanding so that gradually, your old *samskaras*, wrong beliefs, wrong tendencies, wrong habits, which have got a firm root by now, starts diluting and dissolving.

The forthcoming chapters of the book are devoted to giving you this right understanding about life which will become the base of your journey towards freedom.

■■■

How to Remain Ever Free

1

Freedom from the Past

One of the reasons due to which we lose much of the joy in our life is that most of the time, we remain in the past. We float in the past on three accounts:

Most of the people remain immersed in the memories of the past and miss the present.

1. We constantly dream of whatever good and pleasant has occurred to us in the past and remain immersed in those memories and scenes and wish the same to be repeated in future in the same form or in a more exciting form. So you can see that the future is nothing but the projection of our past.

2. Whatever bad or unpleasant has happened to us in the past, constantly trouble us and we keep asking ourselves as to why it happened to me or why was I so unlucky? You also feel shuddered to imagine

those incidents which were heart-rending/shocking and tragic.

3. If something wrong or undesirable has been done by you in the past due to your fault or negligence the past (whether from social, legal or moral consideration), it constantly moves with you like a sword hanging above your head in the form of guilt. [More about 'Guilt' in chapter 46.]

Now think whether any of the above serves some purpose or it simply spoils the joy of our present also. The point no.1 mentioned above simply makes you more and more excited because you want to repeat those pleasures of the past but **life never repeats itself. Repetition is not the law of the universe. Here every moment comes as a fresh package.** The point no.2 mentioned above makes you simply depressed by thinking about the bad things which happened to you and the third point keeps you in a state of guilt.

From spiritual perspective, we should continuously die to the past whether good or bad and be reborn in the present. After dealing with a moment fully and wholeheartedly, we should be able to let it go and welcome the next moment. No clinging should remain with the moment which is passing away. Swami Vivekananda always used to emphasise that concentration and detachment should be practised simultaneously. This is actually the key of spirituality, i.e., **concentration on the present moment and detachment from the past moment**. Of course, consciously recalling some information of the past from your memory for making its use in the present is a different thing and this shouldn't be confused with what we are talking about.

Please remember that spiritually, the only use of the past is to learn various lessons which various situations and events have presented before you. The actual events are not that important. Regarding your attachment to the pleasures of the past, please note that God has designed this life and this world in such a manner that pleasures and joys are not concentrated in a particular time and in a particular place. They are scattered across all times and all spaces. So instead of clinging on to the old pleasures of the past, enjoy the fresh and new pleasures of the present, otherwise in the attempt to hold on to the past, you will continuously miss the joys and pleasures of the present and therefore, will not be able to live your life to the fullest.

■■■

Freedom from the Future

We, particularly Indians, remain very much interested to know as to what lies in our future. We don't want to see what is there in front of us at this very moment. We are more interested to see and know what is behind the curtain which cannot be seen and known directly.

*People immersed in future day dreaming
often end up in being a frustrated lot.*

We keep on meeting astrologers, palmists, numerologists, face readers, voice readers and what not, just to know what will happen in the future and in this process, constantly miss the beauty and joy of the present. So what is there in our hands, also slips out in the quest to know what is not in our hands. In fact, when future comes, you will miss that particular moment also because you will be looking into the further future because of your mindset.

And it is a harsh fact of life that no matter where you go, future still remains open and unknown. It can't be fully known by the very nature of life. So what is the alternative left for you? The alternative is that rejoice in the present and welcome the unknown. Take the unknown as an adventure. As in any kind of adventurous game, you curiously await the next moment with excitement and thrill and not with depression; the same attitude should be displayed in your day-to-day life. Another attitude which you should develop is that put more attention on what is there in front of you, rather than on what is hidden from you. So, enjoy and relish each moment fully without too much worrying about the next moment. Deal with the next moment when it comes.

Even common sense also dictates that it is foolish to spoil our present in the anticipation of some bad event in the future. **Even if something bad is going to occur in future, at least enjoy your life upto that moment. Suffer only when the real suffering comes**. Why do you want to suffer before the real suffering actually comes?

Also keep in mind that like your life until now, your future will also be a mixture of good and bad, pleasant and unpleasant. Nothing special is going to happen in the future. And as you have faced good and bad until now, you can face the same in future also. You should assert mentally that whatever is going to come in future, you will accept it and face it with all your courage and ability and with full faith in God. There is nothing which you can't face and solve with the help of God. In fact, **there is a divine law that God gives problems along with solutions and He never gives more than what we can bear**.

And the miracle is that the only way to make your future better is to be alert and conscious in the present and to take care of the present as well as you can. **Future is made out of your present only. Future is nothing but an extension of your present moment only. In fact, you never** meet the future directly. **Future comes to you only in the form of present. Future continually keeps on turning into the present**. Please note that future is not made by the Almighty randomly. He carefully weaves your future from your past and present, keeping in mind your needs and lessons to learn. So from this angle, you, yourself are the creator of your future and nobody else.

■■■

Freedom from Doership Attitude

We, human beings, somehow tend to believe that we are the doers of whatever we are doing. However, if we contemplate deeply, we will find that every action in the world, no matter however small, involves so many factors and uncertainties that it is impossible for a human being to claim the doership and proprietorship for any activity.

Doership attitude indicates the strong ego in the person.

We fail to see that ultimately everything is being controlled by a **Higher Power or what we term as 'God'**. If that Higher power doesn't want a thing to happen, you may work day and night like a donkey but nothing will happen. In short, the complete control of all the factors which lead to the fruition of a work can only be in the hands of God and not with any human being. Human beings are very tiny and powerless entities in the vast machinery of the universe which is being controlled by a much Higher Power.

What we mean to conclude by this is that we should leave the ego of doership of any action and work only as a *Nimmit* or a servant of God clearly realizing in mind that though we are doing our best according to the resources and freedom available with us but ultimately, everything is in the hands of God or the Almighty. If His support is not there, nothing will materialize in spite of our best efforts.

With this attitude, all your actions become divine because of being free from ego. It is the ego which adulterates and makes your actions impure. In this egoless state, you always feel light while performing any action and never burdened with the tension of the outcome of your actions because once you are not the doer, you don't bother about the results also. Results are left in the hands of God. If the results are good, you surrender them to God with all humility and thankfulness, never taking the credit for that on yourself. In other words, your ego doesn't swell with the positive results. It remains untouched by the awards of work.

People, who consider themselves the doer always remain burdened with the load of responsibilities over their shoulders and are always worried whether the desired result will come or not. Because they have taken everything over their head. They don't want to leave anything in the hands of God. On the other hand, a person who works in association with God, leaving the real doership and results in the hands of God feels always light and unburdened. He doesn't carry unnecessary responsibilities over his head.

■ ■ ■

Freedom from Superiority and Inferiority Complex

What is **Superiority Complex**? It means that "I am superior to others". One interesting point regarding superiority complex is that the existence of others is a must for claiming superiority. Suppose by sheer chance, you are left alone on this earth. Can you then have any feeling of superiority complex? So the first thing to know is that superiority complex is always based on comparison with others. Without 'others', it can't stand alone by itself. It simply drops dead. Now anything for the existence of which you are dependent on others, cannot have any stability of its own.

Superiority Complex is damaging to the development of your consciousness.

Superiority complex is a negative quality, an attribute of ego or your 'Lower Nature'. Since it is based on comparison,

21

it will always be shaky because anytime a person more superior to you can appear. And for ego, it is very difficult to accept that anybody is superior to it.

Now spirituality says that our feeling of superiority should not be based on comparison with others. You should be confident in yourself that you are capable of doing a thing, that you can handle such and such project, that you have such and such calibre without any reference of any other person. This is called the quality of 'Self-confidence' and is an attribute of 'Higher Nature' as compared to the quality of 'Superiority complex' which is an attribute of 'Lower Nature' or ego.

Spirituality further points out that since the ultimate potential of every person is the same which resides in your 'inner Self', so there is no point in comparing yourself with anybody. It is only a question of awakening of this potential from the 'inner Self' by various spiritual practices.

Like Superiority Complex, 'Inferiority Complex' is also based on comparison with others. Here you feel that you are inferior to others. You feel that you can't do what others can do. So, it is the same problem as Superiority Complex but simply 'upside down'. The arguments given above for the falsity of Superiority Complex are equally valid to prove the falsity of Inferiority Complex. The bottom line is that *one should neither feel superior nor inferior to anybody* and have the feeling that "I can do what others can do and others can do what I can do". We are all equal in our ultimate potential.

■■■

Freedom from Ownership Attitude

Most of us have the illusion that whatever we have, we are the owners of it and have our exclusive right and propriety on it. We don't realize that what we are having today, belonged to somebody else in the past (in the same or another form) and in the future also, these things will pass on to somebody else either directly by us while we are alive or indirectly after our death. We have come empty handed in the world at the time of our birth and will go empty handed at the time of our death.

Ownership attitude is a hindrance in your development.

Even when we are alive, the nature of life is such that anything can be taken away from us anytime either by natural means (e.g. natural calamities like earthquakes, floods, cyclones, etc.) or manmade calamities (wars, looting, terrorism, murder, thefts, dacoity, etc.)

In fact, the world by its very nature is impermanent, transient and ever-changing. It is like a river which is always flowing. Nothing can remain static or permanent here by the very nature of life. In such a scenario, claiming ownership and making rigid boundaries around things owned by us is like living in a dream which can be shattered anytime leaving us shocked, embarrassed and miserable.

The right attitude to the things and possessions you have is that they belong to God. God has given them to you for your use for a certain period of time for which you should show gratefulness to God and accept them humbly; and whenever God wants to take them back through any means, you should gladly let them go and release them from your hands as lightly as a balloon is released in air. With this attitude, your attachment to your possessions will gradually weaken and you will always remain light, cheerful and filled with the feelings of thankfulness towards God.

■■■

Freedom from Blind Faith and Conditioning

This is one of the fundamental requirements for our spiritual growth that we should be free from any kind of blind faith, conditioning and programming by others. We should never

Getting immediately influenced and conditioned by an advertisement or suggestion is not a sign of developed mind

get carried away by others' suggestions, advertisements and repetitive hammering of certain ideas on our mind. If we get influenced easily by others, it is akin to getting hypnotised and is highly detrimental to our development.

In fact, it is said that spirituality is more a process of deletion rather than adding into you. You have to first get dehypnotised, deconditioned from everything and become a clean slate. Then only something useful can be put there. Instead of accepting anything blindly, we should try to understand and weigh everything from our own mind and observations and then come to our own conclusions. **If we really want to grow in a proper manner, we should work on facts and not on beliefs**. Truth need not be borrowed from someone. You should be able to find your own truth, because you have also got the same faculties inside you which Gautam Buddha or any great person had.

But one thing is to be strictly kept in mind that you should also not disbelieve anything straightaway. This is another extreme. This is also not a scientific approach. A true scientist neither believes nor disbelieves anything, he simply examines the things from his own eyes. In case, it fits into his test of truth, he gladly accepts it no matter who has said. **He is neither against nor in favour of anybody. He is simply with the truth and facts**.

The same thing has to be followed while reading books, religious *shastras* and *granthas*. You don't have to believe in something because it is uttered by a great person or prescribed in a holy book. Just read, think, examine and understand with an open mind before accepting and believing anything. Once, you accept something by understanding, then it no more remains a borrowed knowledge. It becomes your own acquired knowledge.

Please also note that when you get biased/prejudiced or conditioned by believing something straightaway or taking something for granted, strong impressions or *samskaras* are deposited in your subconscious mind which veil your 'inner Self' and doesn't allow its light to shine forth. On the other hand, truth or facts don't create any *samskaras* or coverings over your 'inner Self' but help to unveil its beauty.

■■■

Freedom from Imitation

Imitation is one of the dirtiest things to do if you want to grow spiritually. Imitation implies that you have lost your soul. You have lost your own discrimination, your own power of observation and experience. You have lost your eyes and you are walking behind somebody. Wherever he takes you, you go. Whatever he says to believe and do, you believe and do. In short, you lose your dignity as an independent human being in this situation and become dependent on somebody else.

Following somebody blindly may hinder your personal growth.

Spirituality warns that no matter how enlightened a person may be, you should not follow or imitate him blindly. You should maintain your originality and dignity as an individual.

You can listen to a person, read his writings but you shouldn't blindly follow him without understanding and experimenting on your own. You should weigh the thing with your own intellect and discrimination, and also experiment on the experimental part of it, if any, and then make your own conclusions. If you are not able to understand a thing fully at your present level of intellect and understanding, then suspend the judgement, neither right nor wrong. It may be right. It may be wrong. It may be partially right or partially wrong. All possibilities are open which you should experiment, enquire and think about. **However, final conclusions about anything has to be yours. They shouldn't be blindly followed or stolen from somewhere. Following somebody without understanding is a great impediment in your spiritual growth.**

■■■

Freedom from Attachment to Physical Pleasures and Comforts

There have been various religious sects and cults in our country who have taught their followers/*sanyasis*/monks/ nuns to renounce worldly pleasures and comforts and to abhor them. They even claim that it is a sin to give pleasure and comforts to the *Indriyas* (senses) of the body. They call it *Bhoga* and they advise that the *Indriyas* or senses should be deprived and starved of their pleasures. Only then, they can remain pure and in control. Some have gone to the extent of torturing their bodies and *Indriyas* in the name of penance (*Tapasya*).

One should try to enjoy more of 'Satwik' sensual pleasure than 'Rajasik' and 'Tamasik' sensual pleasures.

Nothing can be farther from truth. If pleasures and comforts were undesirable for the body, God would not have given appropriate senses in our body to enjoy them

29

at the first place. In fact, suppression of natural pleasures and comforts can be disastrous for our body. It may lead to unnecessary perversions and various psychological problems.

Now what is wrong is not the enjoyment of pleasures and comforts but attachment to them, over indulgence/ addiction to them, constant thinking and talking about them. You should enjoy them when the need and right moment is there and then let it go. You should not keep on ruminating about them in your thoughts and imagination. That is what attachment is.

Another thing to be kept in mind is that there are two kinds of pleasures: **Lower pleasures** and **Higher pleasures**. Lower pleasures should definitely be avoided and controlled as they are harmful to the body and mind. It is only the enjoyment of Higher pleasures that are worth talking about. Now what are Higher and Lower pleasures?

Higher pleasures are also called *Satwik pleasures*. They are related to the pure Nature and its five elements (*Akasa*, Air, Water, *Agni* and Earth). Below are some of the examples of different kinds of *Satwik pleasures*:

1. You are taking a morning walk in fresh air.

2. You are lying in a garden seeing the sky, the greenery, the birds and hearing their sounds.

3. You are sitting and enjoying the winter sun.

4. You are sitting near a lake/river/waterfall/sea beach, hearing the sound of the moving water, bathing in the natural waters, etc.

5. You are in a hill station, enjoying the natural scenery of the mountains, forests, waterfalls, rivers flowing in the valleys, etc.

6. Listening to a soothing music (e.g. classical music, devotional songs/*bhajans* and other melodious songs.

In short, when we are close to nature, we enjoy *Satwik pleasures*. Similarly, Lower pleasures are *Rajasik and Tamsik* in nature. For example:

1. Eating stimulating foods (spicy, fried, non-veg, etc.)

2. Hearing stimulating songs and music (like modern pop, disco, rock music, etc.)

3. Seeing sensational movies (containing horror, sex, violence, suspense, etc.)

4. Moving in glamorous markets, shopping malls, fairs & exhibitions, etc., displaying lot of pomp and show.

5. Taking narcotic drugs, both stimulating (like Amphetamines) and tranquilizers (like Barbiturates) and Euphoric (like LSD).

6. Smoking, drinking alcohol, intake of tobacco, tea, coffee, cold drinks, etc.

Further, you must distinguish between the basic bodily needs/comforts and sensual pleasures mentioned above. Comforts relate to the body's basic survival needs which must be met. You may call them 'neutral pleasures' (neither positive like *Satwik* nor negative like *Rajasik/Tamsik*). For example, satisfaction of thirst or hunger is just a basic necessity of the body. You can't call them pleasures in a strict sense. Similarly, when you go for natural calls in the morning after having a pressure (defecation and urination), you get relief and comfort after you release the pressure. You cannot strictly call it a pleasure. Similarly, suppose, you are feeling discomfort in hot summer. You come inside a room fitted with a cooler. You feel comfortable. You simply come from a position of discomfort to comfort. So these are all basic bodily needs and comforts. You can't call them lower or higher pleasures or good and bad. Only thing is that you can fulfil these comforts in a healthy or an unhealthy way. For example, suppose you are feeling thirsty. Now you can quench the thirst by drinking natural water or by chilled ice water from the fridge or by taking Cola drinks. Chilled ice water or Cola drinks are not a healthy choice. It has some harmful effects. Similarly, you are feeling hungry. You can eat a simple food (cereals, dal, vegetable, etc.) or you can satisfy your hunger by taking junk food also (e.g. pizza, burger, chips, ice cream, etc.) which is an unhealthy choice.

■■■

Freedom from Impulse and Reaction

Normally our attitude in life is like this that if anybody says or does anything bad to us whether real or apparent, we immediately react with an impulsive and attacking attitude. It is as if someone has touched a button inside us which has immediately activated us like a robot or a mechanical device. This is what impulse or reaction is. This is the normal tendency of our ego or Lower nature.

One must develop enough tolerance and patience to live peacefully.

Maturity consists in not reacting to anything immediately based on Lower nature impulses but allow sometime to pass and then respond consciously. Our intellect has basically two faculties in it:

33

1. Reasoning, logical analysis

2. Will power or control or mental strength

With the help of 'will power' or 'control', you delay your reaction (or Lower nature impulse) and in the intervening time, you decide the proper response with the help of your reasoning faculty. This is called conscious response as against unconscious reaction in the first case. Your conscious response may include telling someone assertively his wrong acts or remarks and your strong disliking about that or your conscious response may be simply to remain silent because you feel that the issue is not worth discussing. Further a person may not be at that level where he will appreciate your reasoning and mend himself. In fact, whenever you feel that a discussion will be a wastage of time and energy because the other person is too biased or conditioned to appreciate your view point, it is better to remain silent and find some other solution rather than involving in confrontation and long arguments.

It is also to be noted that a person who is in a hot mood and full of negative emotions, will also not be able to appreciate your reasoning in that state of mind. To understand and appreciate the reasoning, one has to have a cool mind. Allowing sometime to pass enables the other person also to come to a relatively cool state.

Whenever you exercise such tolerance and patience against some provocating situation, your mental strength and will power increases which helps you to exercise control and patience more easily in similar types of incidents in future. When your mental strength is sufficiently increased, then you will not feel very much shaken or perturbed or uncontrolled by bad or unreasonable things being done by others to you. You will feel like a rock on whom waves are hitting yet it remains stable.

■■■

Freedom from Doubt and Mistrust

Having trust and faith in others is a divine virtue held by spiritually developed and mature people. This has nothing to do whether others are really good or bad. Jesus Christ used to say, **"Even if the other person is bad and a cheat, still why do you want to lose the joy which trust and faith gives?"** Another quote by a great soul says **"It is better to be deceived than mistrust a person."**

Doubt and suspicion eats you like termites.

There are people who start their interactions by always doubting the bonafides of other person. This is a very negative approach. Spiritual approach is that don't start with the preconceived bias in your mind that the other person is a cheat and will definitely deceive you and loot you. Start with faith. Even after having faith, if a person cheats you, he is actually cheating himself, first. He suffers much more for this act according to the law of *Karma* than the harm done by him to you. Any person doing good or bad to you will automatically enjoy or suffer according to the divine laws whether you punish him or not. Why do you bother for that? No person can ever escape from any evil deed done by him, whether this evil deed has been done under the sea or above the sky.

However, by creating a balance between spiritual philosophy and practical life, you can at least adopt this principle that **you will consider every person good unless he proves himself otherwise**. That is to say that initially, you should never mistrust a person. Only when a person proves himself otherwise by his activities, you can lose your faith on him.

■■■

Freedom from Making Judgements

If we observe our behaviour in day-to-day life, we will find that we are an expert in making judgements about people whether somebody is good or bad, honest or corrupt, fast or gentle, clever or innocent. And then our judgements also go on varying with time. Somebody whom we have certified good now, we can declare him bad after one month if he

*Making judgement about the whole community
based on a single experience is immature.*

hasn't fulfilled our wish or not favoured or helped us in some matter. So much fragile our judgements are. **Another funny thing in our judgements is that whether we are good or not but we are always ready to decide whether the other person is good or bad.**

Spirituality advises us that we should be non-judgemental and non-critical. **Except God and an enlightened person, nobody has the right to judge and pass verdict on any person.** Moreover, to judge a person, first your level has to be higher than him. But there are people who stand nowhere in character and they are passing verdict on Mahatma Gandhi, Mother Teresa, Shankaracharya and so on. And the surprising thing is that an enlightened person who has the right to judge, never makes any judgemental remark against any person. He simply helps you to grow no matter at what level you are.

Further, you should also realize whether any good will result after you make a judgement. Suppose, you say that a person is bad, will he become good after hearing your statement? My understanding is that after hearing your remarks, he may become more egoistic and resistant to leave his badness. So even if somebody is really bad, corrupt and dishonest, then instead of making judgements and remarks, you should find indirect ways by which his badness may not get a chance to sprout and come forth so that the damage to the society is reduced.

■■■

Freedom from the Fear of Death

Death is a very natural phenomena of life and anything which is as per natural laws is neither painful nor to be feared. Death is just a transition from one life to another, a time for rest and self evaluation between two lives. After death, you are just the same as before except that you don't have a physical body and you reside in the **Astral world** which is at a different vibratory frequency than the **Physical world**.

> What will happen when I will be dying?

Fear of death sucks all your energy of living.

In fact, death is not a problem. It is the thought of death which is a problem. Real death is just like dozing off to sleep. Only difference is that in ordinary sleep, you wake up in the same body, while in death, you wake up in another body (Astral Body). So if you don't think about death and just let it happen whenever it occurs, then all the horror and fear of death vanishes.

Many people fear death thinking that it entails a lot of suffering and pain. But this notion is far from truth. The fact is contrary. Suffering and pain exist only till you are alive. **Death is the cessation of all the suffering or pain**. That's why you might have observed that no matter how much pain or suffering a person is having before death but after the moment of death, if you look at the face of the person, it seems relaxed and peaceful. I still remember the beautiful quote of a person on death "**It is impossible that anything so natural, so necessary and so universal as death should ever have been designed by providence as an evil to mankind.**"

Ignorant people think of death as an unfortunate event as if something bad has happened to the dying person while, in fact, reverse is the case. The dying person is relieved of the sufferings which he was undergoing while being alive. Ofcourse, the amount of suffering which a person undergoes before death, while being alive, is a totally different matter and is dependent on a complex network of *Karma*. From this angle, one person may die without any presuffering while another person may go on suffering a lot and still he may not die. In fact, according to the philosophy of *Karma*, unless a person undergoes his *karmically* determined sufferings fully in life, nature will not allow him to die. He will go on escaping death somehow.

Another thing to be noted is that the length of life upto death is not important. The important thing is the quality of life upto the time of death, i.e., how beautifully you have lived each moment of your life upto death.

People who have reached to a very high level of consciousness die a conscious death, i.e., they can visualize that they are being separated from the body without losing consciousness, while ordinary people become totally unconscious during the process of death when the immortal soul leaves the mortal body.

Freedom from Revenge

Normally, when a person does anything bad to you, e.g., suppose somebody deceives you, your immediate reaction is to take a revenge and do greater harm to him, a kind of reflex action from our Lower nature or ego.

Revenge is a never ending game.

However, spirituality points out that **revenge is such a game in which players die but the game never ends**. Hence, spirituality advises us to develop the attitude of 'forget and forgive' for the ills done by others to you. Forgiveness acts as a soothing balm for your burning heart and makes you immediately light and free. **It doesn't matter whether the other person deserves forgiveness or not but at least, you deserve your freedom of mind. The burden of hatred and malice which you carry on your head by not forgiving someone, harms you much more than that person.**

Forgiveness means completely forgetting and burning the issue forever. If you say that you can forgive, but cannot forget, it means that you haven't forgiven and you have simply repressed the matter beneath your conscious mind. Example of Jesus Christ who had forgiven even those who were responsible for his crucification is the highest and a praiseworthy example of forgiveness.

If you have this feeling in your mind as to how the person who has done ill to you will realize his mistake and get punished, then please remember that it is not you who can adequately punish a person. Right punishment at the right time always comes from God which nobody can escape. So by your forgiveness, the punishment from God's side has not been over. Everybody has to unerringly settle his accounts with God.

■■■

Freedom from Attachment to the Body

Reason for the attachment to the body is that we deeply identify ourselves with our bodies and almost think that we are nothing but bodies. However, the fact is that the body is simply your possession like you possess a car, a house or a motorcycle. You are the soul or consciousness which is different from the body and only lives in the body and uses it for sometime. You simply own the body.

Attachment to the body keeps you in great anxiety.

Your body is material but your soul is non-material. Your body comes from your parents while your soul comes from somewhere else and simply enters the body after conception. Your body is perishable but your soul is eternal.

43

Once you are clear of this difference and separation between you (i.e. the soul) and the body (your possession), then the attachment to the body will easily reduce.

You should utilize this knowledge in your practical life also. Suppose your body gets injured, you should clearly feel that you are not injured, it is the body which is injured. You are simply a watcher standing at a distance and seeing the body injured. Similarly, if you get some disease in the body, you should clearly feel that you are not diseased. It is the body which is diseased and you are watching the disease as a separate entity.

This practice of constant awareness of separation between the soul and the body will decrease your attachment towards the body and thereby reduce various psychological sufferings such as fear, worries, etc., which you endure just because of your deep identification with the body or considering yourself the body itself.

■■■

Freedom from Hurry

If you observe around you, you will find that some people always remain in a hurry whether it is needed or not. It becomes a tendency or a mindset for them. They somehow want to hurriedly finish the work in hand, so that they can relax in some imaginary future. But when that moment comes, they can't relax because their future oriented and rushing attitude continues and can't be suddenly changed. This rushing attitude is always reflected on their tense face in the form of wrinkles.

Hurry keeps you in perpetual tension.

Now why people remain in a hurry? Because they are not happy in the present. If you are happy, fully satisfied and contented in the present, why will you think of rushing to a future moment? In this process of thinking ahead of the time, we actually neglect the present and spend our time

45

right now in unhappiness. It is our future oriented and rushing mind which blocks our happiness of the present moment and keeps our mind constantly agitated.

The solution is to learn to stop yourself in the present moment. Once you learn to slow down your mind to the activity in hand, you will find that the most ordinary and mundane works, which earlier used to be quite boring, become quite interesting and a source of great joy and satisfaction.

It is only by slowing down and paying attention to each moment that many of the things happening around us which are normally taken for granted and seem dull and uninteresting, become highly interesting and enjoyable. If we want to experience joy and happiness in our works, we should leave the attitude of rushing through our activities and to somehow finish them as early as possible. This should be replaced by an attitude of slowing down and maintaining full awareness in each activity, however trivial it may be. If we are not mindful in each small activity, we can't be mindful in carrying out important tasks also because our attitude and the frame of mind can't be suddenly changed.

■■■

Freedom from Obsession with Gurus

Freedom from *Gurus* (or spiritually enlightened Masters) doesn't imply that we should leave them or become against them or speak ill of them. As I have also explained in chapter 17, it only means that **we shouldn't become overly fanatic, possessive and obsessive about them**. They shouldn't become the cause of our quarrel and separation from each other. We frequently observe in India that people

Blind faith in a Guru can do more harm than good.

following one *Guru* will become one separatist group and the people following another *Guru* will form another separatist group and they become antagonist to each other because one will claim that his *Guru* is superior and the other will claim that his *Guru* is superior. One will claim what his *Guru* is right and the other will say that his *Guru* is always right. This is how religious wars and antagonisms begin.

In this connection, please note that *Gurus* are only spiritual teachers to help you and guide you in your spiritual growth. Your aim should be that you should get from them as much help as you can for your spiritual journey. Your aim is not to attach to them. Your attachment should be with your ultimate goal which is God. In fact, no real *Guru* will encourage you to be overly attached to him. Gautam Buddha used to say to his disciples that "If in meditation, you see me instead of God, then immediately kill me". This instruction was to emphasize the above referred point only.

The enlightened Master, Osho says "**After a certain point in your spiritual journey, a Guru becomes a hindrance instead of help**". This is because once you are able to stand on your own feet, a *Guru* is no more required. Hence, a real *Guru* will set you free at this stage and will encourage you to find your own path. That is why, the same enlightened Master Osho says, "***Guru* is a necessary evil in the beginning**". This is because initially, *Guru* is very much required because you are totally in darkness but afterwards, if you insist on sticking to him, you will not be able to reach to your ultimate goal because your journey will stop in your *Guru* rather than in God.

You must understand that your ultimate goal is God and not the *Guru*. A *Guru* is simply a teacher or a help to reach your goal which is God. Another thing, which is important for you is to understand that you should not blindly believe and follow what your *Guru* is saying. You must apply your own mind and thought to understand what is being taught to you. You must observe in terms of your own experiences as to how a thing or practice is appealing to your heart and benefiting you. **Blindly following somebody with a**

48

closed mind can be a great pitfall in your spiritual journey.

Please keep in mind that the ultimate truth has to be found by you personally. Truth can't be borrowed or copied. Your *Guru's* truth can't be your truth. It has to be experienced by you personally. Once, you experience it, you also become a *Guru* in your own right and no more a follower of your earlier *Guru*. That is why it said that a **real Guru prepares Gurus like himself while a false Guru creates disciples and followers.**

■■■

Freedom from Obsession with Religious Scriptures

Freedom from religious scriptures doesn't mean that you should hate them or throw them or find fault with them. What we mean to say by this phrase is that you should not be overly attached or obsessed or overly possessive about them. You must respect, study and learn as much as you can from the religious scriptures with an open mind but should not become a fanatic about them and they should not become the cause of quarrel and separation between different religions.

Fighting over superiority of one's own religious scripture leads to no result.

But what we observe in real life is that people are just doing the opposite. They are not reading the scriptures and taking necessary lessons from them for improving their life but they are simply possessive and protective about them.

50

Everyone draws a boundary wall around his/her religion in which persons of other religions should not intrude and should not dare to make any adverse comment about his/her religion or religious scripture. And if anybody dares to do that, immediately the swords are drawn out, and wars and violence begin. **Hence, it has been rightly said that the maximum wars in the world have been fought in the name of religion**.

Another funny thing which is observed in our society is that people of one religion don't study the religious scriptures of another religion though all of them contain the highest truths uttered by their respective enlightened *Gurus*. This creates separation among different religious groups while the basic purpose of all the religions is to join, to create unity and to remove separation. So here lies the fallacy.

Now the right approach is that **instead of keeping their respective religious scriptures under lock and key and daily removing their dust, one should study them (or their commentary by different scholars), try to grasp and understand the essence of what is written** and if one finds something appealing and useful one must apply them in one's practical life. Actually, one should not only study the scripture of one's own religion but should also study the scriptures of other religions (and their commentary). If you do so, you will find many useful things in them also because they also contain the message of their Masters who were as enlightened as the founders of your own religion. At the highest level, there is no difference between one *Guru* and the another. Then you should also exchange the views on different matters with persons of different religions with an open and scientific mind without any religion bias or idea of separatism.

People of different religions should freely mingle with each other and exchange their view points contained in their holy scriptures and in their Master's voice. Little difference in ideology and philosophy shouldn't become the reason for quarrel and disputes. One should develop enough tolerance to accommodate the differences without any fight and ill will towards each other. In fact, **the ultimate truth has to be found out by you yourself and is not to be copied or borrowed blindly from these religious scriptures**. The various religious scriptures and the Master's words of different religions are to be used only as a guidance or help in your own search towards the truth. They are not to be followed blindly in toto without understanding.

■■■

Freedom from Expectations

Expecting from others is one of the great causes of sorrow in life. The reason being that what we expect from others is rarely fulfilled. It has to be so by the very nature of life. We normally expect from others in the following situations:

I never expected that you will give such a cheap gift on my b'day. I always give so beautiful and costly gifts on every occasion.

Expectation leads to sourness in our relationships.

1. When we have given something to someone or done some favour or help to someone.

2. When we have entered into some sort of social relationship with someone (e.g. marriage and various other relations like brother-sister relation, father-son relation, uncle-nephew relation, sister-sister relation, cousin brothers and sisters relations,

grandfather-grandson relation, aunt-niece relation and so on). There are expectations from each relation based on the duties and norms fixed by our society for each type of relation.

3. When we develop attachment with some specific person due to love with him/her. In such a case, you develop the expectation that he should meet you frequently, write to you and phone you frequently, be available whenever you miss him or whenever you are sick or in some problem. But all this may not be practically possible for him/her every time due to which you suffer from lots of mental agony. Even the other person also feels that you have bound him and his freedom is being lost.

Now if you contemplate deeply, you will realize that these types of expectations are a type of bargaining where one is obliged to give you something in return in proportion to what you have given or done. And if he doesn't give, you will feel continuously bad against him. In social relationships, if you don't do something for someone as per the norms of the society, then there will be ill-will among the relations.

There is a strange paradox in the philosophy of fulfillment of expectations that it is never practically possible for anyone to fulfil all the expectations of another person even if one wants to do so because of the very nature of life which doesn't allow the same to happen as the expectations are endless like a chain. If you fulfil one expectation of somebody, another expectation will arise and if you don't fulfil this other expectation the person will still be annoyed with you as if you have done nothing for him. The situation is like a holed bucket of water which never gets filled up no matter how much you put in.

Then should we live constantly in the state of resentment against each other for not fulfilling our expectations?

No, this is not necessary. Spirituality gives us the right understanding in this matter to solve the dilemma. According to the spiritual principles, our joy should come right from giving and not from receiving. There is a great joy in giving and we should discover this joy of giving. The joy of selfless giving is so much that who cares for receiving. But why are we not able to discover this joy? It is primarily because of two reasons:

1. Even before we give to others, we start thinking about what we will get in return. This immediately destroys the joy of giving.

2. Before you give, you must have enough. Suppose, you want to give joy and happiness to someone and you don't have it inside you. Then the result will be misery. We start thinking to give to others without realizing whether we ourselves have enough.

So the point is that first have enough with yourself whatever you want to give and secondly, start experiencing the joy of giving instead of looking for receiving. This will be one of the greatest discoveries of your life and you will find that all your frustrations of expectations from others have vanished into the air. You should also understand that the various relationships in our society is a social phenomena made for the convenience of the society. It has nothing to do with spirituality. In spirituality, everybody is an independent human being and a unique individual having equal relationship with each other.

There are few more things to be noted regarding expectations:

(i) When you expect something from someone and the person fulfils your expectation, then you don't give it much value and take it for granted because you already expected it from him and you feel he has done nothing special. But if you don't expect anything from somebody and still he does something

55

for you, you become greatly pleased and obliged. So you can see that through expectation, you lose the joy of receiving.

(ii) In expectations, you become dependent on another person because you are at the mercy of the other person. There is no guarantee that the other person will fulfil your expectation. It is his free-will whether he fulfils your expectation or not. You can't force him. And this dependency always creates misery.

(iii) In the case of attachment with the specific person due to the development of love with him (the 3rd category of expectation as listed in the beginning), spirituality discourages attachment with a specific person or a thing. Spirituality aims at love and attachment for all and not with specifics.

In the end, the conclusion is that try to be independent and self sufficient in life as far as possible and don't depend on others for those things which you can do by yourself. In case anybody does something for you on his own, be grateful to him but don't expect. However, when you require any genuine help from somebody be frank and liberal in asking for the same but don't expect him to offer help to you on his own. Show gratefulness if the other agrees for providing help to you. If he refuses, don't feel resentful but go to some other person for help. Similarly, when somebody needs help from you, be ever ready to help (provided it is within your resources ad capability) irrespective of who is asking. There should be no discrimination that you will help only your friends and not others. As mentioned earlier, in spirituality your relationship with everybody is same. There is nobody close or far. Everybody deserves your love and help equally without any discrimination.

Freedom from Religion, Caste, Creed and Nationality

In this world, we find people born in different religions, caste, creed and nationality. This should not matter if the people can enjoy this diversity by intermingling freely among each other, exchanging and enjoying each other's customs, rituals, culture and then learn and take from others what is useful and worth adopting from their culture. In other words, **we should be able to find a thread of unity between this diversity and variety** instead of living in isolated compartments as islands.

I believe only in Hinduism. Only this religion can liberate us.

Fanatism with a particular religion
is a great stumbling block in your progress.

Problem comes when we make rigid walls around our religions, customs, caste, nations and always remain apprehensive about those who are outside these walls, not allowing their free entry into our premises. People who dare to enter into our heavily guarded fortress for having a free dialogue with us are threatened by us and sometimes, we rage a war against them.

So problem is not diversity or variety in this world. In fact, the **diversity in the world is as beautiful as different types of flowers in a garden**. The main problem comes when we make this diversity ugly by making rigid boundaries and divisions which create the illusion of separateness. This separateness creates a feeling of discomfort, disease and feeling of alienation and antagonism with other separatist groups. And because of this feeling of separateness, we become highly possessive, protective, obsessive and fanatic about our religion, caste, nationality and start fighting even if someone shows slight disagreement and difference with the ideology and philosophy of our religion.

While in reality, the differences between the ideology and philosophy of different religions should give an opportunity for wider discussions so as to come to a more holistic truth. **Truth is not a rigid thing confined to the ideology of one religion. Different religions provide an opportunity for reaching to a more cumulative nature of truth**.

No religious founder had ever this feeling that his followers should make a separatist group in his name with antagonism to another religion. Swami Vivekanand has beautifully depicted this spirit by saying that "**Different religions flourishing in our country should be complementary to each other, benefiting from each other rather than becoming antagonist to each other**".

You can compare different kinds of religions to different kinds of schools in which we study. In our schools, we get material education while the religions give us spiritual knowledge of life. As we never get overly attached to different schools in which we study and our sole aim remains to learn or to acuire knowledge, similarly, we shouldn't get overly attached to our religions. Our main aim should be to take the spiritual knowledge from different religions rather than getting identified with them. As we mention the name of our school simply for the sake of information, and not to convey that I am a staunch follower of this school, so should be with the religion. **There is no need to be a strong follower/supporter of a certain religion to learn from it. Rather, overclinging sometimes comes in the way of our unbiased learning**. This true understanding of religion will remove all types of malice between followers of different religions.

■■■

Freedom from Boredom and Loneliness

If we observe ourselves and the people around us, we will find one thing in common that we are not able to remain alone and ourselves anytime. We always want something 'other' with us to keep us occupied and busy. This 'other' may be an object, a person or some scene. Boredom comes from this tendency to remain always with some 'other' and not able to enjoy our aloneness.

We should always find sometime in our life when
we are just ourselves and not engaged with anything else.

Try to observe yourself on some day when you are relatively idle with no work to do and no person around to gossip. Then what do you do? You will either open the television or start reading some newspaper or magazine or just phone somebody to talk without any specific reason or just start eating something whether hungry or not and if these things are also snatched from you, then you feel utterly bored and empty as well as frustrated. **You constantly seek something 'other' to fill your emptiness. You can't remain happily with yourself alone.**

This is one of the greatest reasons for our unhappiness in life that we always need 'others' and we can't remain without 'others'. **Dependency on others will always create misery since others are always changing and they can also disappear and vanish anytime.** So the miracle is that although we constantly seek 'others' but we also remain miserable with 'others'. Also note that in our choice of 'others' to keep us occupied and avoid boredom, we will always choose a human being in order of priority.

Now the solution of this problem lies in this that we should gradually learn to remain ourselves and cherish and enjoy our loneliness. We should interact and deal with others whenever required but we should leave dependency on 'others'. **You should be able to say that "I can live alone happily. Others are not necessary for my happiness."**

In fact, this is what meditation is all about, i.e., to live with yourself, to relax and rest in yourself. Everyday, no matter how busy you are, just **find sometime when you are absolutely alone. At this time, you are neither a husband nor a wife, neither a father nor a son, neither a boss nor a subordinate, neither a man nor a woman. You are just, 'you'.**

This taste of loneliness or solitude will fill you with a unique joy which can never be experienced in company of others. And the more you taste it, the more you will like to remain with it. It pulls you like a magnet. You will be so addicted to it that you can leave anything but you will not miss this joy. **In fact, this joy is nothing but the joy of your real Self residing inside you. In your aloneness or solitude, you touch this inner Self, hence, you experience so much joy.**

■■■

Freedom from Greed

What is greed? Greed means the desire to accumulate more and more. You are not satisfied with what you have. You always want more. And the miracle is that a greedy person can never feel satisfied no matter how much he is able to

I want a bigger house and want to replace these cars with imported cars having automatic gears.

A greedy person always wants more and more, no matter what he has got.

get because there is no limit of getting. **No matter how much you get, still 'more' remains to be obtained. There is no limit of accumulating the things in this world. That is why you can never quench the thirst of a greedy person.**

Now, how greed originates in the first place. Basically, greed originates in the mind because of the feeling of insecurity. You never know what will happen tomorrow? May be, you become sick. May be your wife/husband dies and your children leave you or you become alone in the world. May be some accident or tragedy occurs leading to a lot of loss.

But the fact of life is that no matter what you do, insecurity still remains. Insecurity is inbuilt in the very fabric of life. It can't be totally removed by any of your efforts. For instance, think that even if you have accumulated much to cater to some imagined problems of the future and the actual problem which comes is of much higher magnitude than your accumulations can cater, then what will you do? **Please note that your permanent security lies only in the hands of God.**

So the wise thing is that do a reasonable planning and saving for catering to needs of the future but don't be unduly skeptical, apprehensive and overcrazy about your security in future. Have a firm faith in God and remember this divine law that God always gives problems along with solutions and never hits one more than what he or she can bear.

■■■

Freedom from Trying to Change Others

If you sometimes look and probe into the psychology of people, you will find that most of the time everybody is thinking in terms of changing others, changing the situations, changing the place of living, changing the job,

Trying to change others forcibly leads to opposite results.

changing the life partner, etc. **Except himself, a person wants to change everything**. And he thinks that by changing others, he will become happy. This attitude is the biggest trap working against your happiness because spirituality says that **Except yourself, you can't change anybody**.

So if we really want to be peaceful and happy, we have to stop thinking in terms of changing others because of two basic reasons:

1. We can't change a person against his desire. Rather the more force, we apply in changing him, the more he becomes adamant not to change by the very nature of ego. Ego always resists any force or imposition.

2. Even if the other person changes, there is no guarantee for your happiness. Your happiness rests entirely in your change.

So even if you are facing some bad persons or bad situations in life, the approach should be how to change or adjust yourself so that their badness and negativity affects you the least. **So instead of changing situations or persons, you have to change your reactions towards them**. There is no direct way to change a bad person or bad situation. It has never happened in the world that you have told a bad person that he should become good and he immediately agreed with you and has become good. Another miracle is that by changing your reactions to a bad person's behaviour, you also help him to change indirectly because once you react differently, he can no longer behave with you in the same fashion. He will have to change his response towards you.

Further, once you change yourself, then the people working around you and interacting with you start getting automatically transformed through the process of induction by observing your way of working, your way of dealing, your balance and stability in adverse circumstances and by the peace and joy which radiates from your personality. Your personality indirectly elevates them without any effort on their part. They start changing even without their knowing. This is how a good company and good environment transforms the people indirectly. **The superior vibrations of an advanced personality and the positive environment around that person also raise the vibrations of those who remain close to them. In the Guru-disciple relationship, this works as a very strong factor. The disciple's vibrations are raised so easily in the presence of his Master that the disciple spontaneously gets transformed by the very proximity to his Master.**

So we come to two important conclusions:

1. There is no direct way to change any person. But there are indirect ways.

2. The only way to change others is to change yourself.

■■■

Freedom from Complaints, Criticisms and Blames

If we look around us, we find that everybody is simply complaining, blaming, criticizing about various systems, departments, people in authority and politics. People constantly complain that everybody is corrupt in government departments and public dealing places

Constant complaining is a sign of low level of consciousness.

including all politicians and ministers; nobody works anywhere and there is lot of lawlessness; Police is shielding the criminals and taking bribes. It sometimes appears from their talks that they are the only clean people in the world and the rest of the world is corrupt while the fact is that if these people are also put in those positions, they will do the same thing. But does this constant bickering and complaining change anything? Yes one thing does happen that it fills your mind with negativity, hatred and ill will during that time when you talk about these things.

Please remember that **complaining and criticizing is not the way to change a bad person or a bad system**. The practical way is to get up from your seat and take some action, whatever is possible within your limitations. For example, you can write letters and reminders to various authorities for any wrongs and malpractices, you notice. You can go in groups to meet various authorities after taking appointments if no action is there on your letters. You can also contact the area MLAs and MPs to put pressure on appropriate authorities. Something will definitely happen by these actions even if not upto your full satisfaction.

In some cases, if you feel that constraints and limitations are such that nothing can be done, then it is better to accept, compromise or adjust rather than constantly weep, criticize and curse yourself and others.

Same is the case when you have to deal with a bad and difficult person in your relation, in your neighbourhood or in your office. Instead of constantly complaining, criticizing, blaming and quarrelling with him for his bad points, try to find indirect ways of dealing with him so that his bad and irritating activities affect you the least or they don't get a chance to erupt. For example, remaining away from him as much as possible and talking to him as little as possible could be some of the possible indirect ways. Please note that by directly complaining, blaming and fighting with a person for his badness, a person becomes more adamant, repulsive and resistant to change because ego is unable to hear and digest its shortcomings even if it is a fact.

Freedom from Pity

Do you know that when you show pity on some person for his condition, what are you saying to him indirectly? You are conveying this message to him "You are unfortunate. You are helpless. Oh poor fellow!" So instead of giving him encouragement to come out of his condition or situation, you are indirectly conveying him that he is a victim. Nothing can be done and he is destined to suffer.

> Oh! What will happen to your family now.

Showing pity to a person in problem can be the worst thing you can do to him.

In our society, we usually think that by showing pity, we are sympathising with the person. **But sympathy and pity are not the same things. In sympathy, we share the sorrow of another person as if it is our sorrow also and help the person to come out of his sad state of affairs.** But by showing pity, we are weakening the person and making him feel that he is a helpless victim of the circumstances and he has no power to do anything.

The spiritual approach is that instead of showing pity on the bad condition of a person, encourage him to take control and responsibility for his condition and develop faith in himself and in God. You have to instal confidence in him that he still has some choices to make. All the doors are never closed for anyone. No matter, how miserable a person is, he can always do something. **This is a wonderful law of life that God never closes all the doors for anyone.**

No matter, how bad a person may have been and in how many limitations, one is living, still everybody is given a chance to grow further and come out of his vicious circle of bondage. No one is doomed to the eternal hell and suffering. Everybody has been given some degree of freedom by God to a higher or lesser degree, depending on one's past *Karmas* to modify his present destiny and improve his future also.

Please note that what has been said above for pitying others, same is true for self pity. You should never feel helpless, unfortunate and a victim when confronted with some misfortune, tragedy, incurable disease or accident. **Instead of blaming others or cursing your luck, you should assume the responsibility for your conditions and circumstances and feel powerful inside to take some actions.**

■■■

Freedom from Bad Luck or Adverse Destiny

Those people who always start cursing their luck at the face of misfortunes, should remember that they are hundred percent responsible for what they are in their life. You make your destiny by your own hands. Your past has made your present. Your present will make your future. What you are experiencing today is the fruit of what you have done in the past. Future is still in your hands if you

Whenever I buy anything, I always end up in losses. I have a very bad luck.

Cursing your luck is an easy escape for many people to avoid personal responsibility.

can be cautious to keep your present in order. Hence, never curse your luck at misfortunes but face the present reality with boldness. **Accepting self responsibility for your life and the realization that your thoughts, words and actions**

are the mould to shape your future, can bring about a major change in your attitude towards life.

Further, you have a power with you by which you can even modify and alter your present destiny. You needn't be a helpless slave in the hands of destiny. By exercising your free will constructively and making actual efforts with firm determination and will power against various obstacles, you can modify the forces of destiny. So destiny is not something rigid. It is constantly subjected to alteration and modification depending upon the use of free will (limited freedom available to you) by you in reacting to your destiny and in generating fresh *karmas*. If you can also surrender yourself to God, then it becomes further easier to detach from the wheel of destiny because of the divine help available to you at every step. Thus, it is not necessary to revolve endlessly in the wheel of destiny like a galley slave. You have the power to come out of this wheel and control it instead of getting controlled by it.

As your level of consciousness rises, the hold of destiny over you goes on loosening and your free will increases. That is why, spiritually enlightened persons are not afraid of destiny at all. They are at a level where they are not moved by the things but they themselves move the things by the use of their increased free will. They have the handle of the wheel of destiny in their hands which they can move as per their will. Destiny works as their servant unlike all of us where destiny works as a master and we, as its servants.

There is another dimension of it also. Once you achieve a high level of consciousness and mental control, you are able to face your adverse destiny boldly. You can withstand it calmly instead of breaking down as it generally happens with weak minded persons. Your reaction and attitude towards adversities of life totally changes. You don't take them seriously and don't question them. You realize that they have come in accordance with certain law and will also disappear after sometime.

■■■

Freedom from Trying to Please and Satisfy Others

Some people make herculean efforts to please and satisfy other people but these people end up being a frustrated lot when in the long run, they find that all their efforts have gone futile and nobody has really been satisfied.

We spend a lot of our energy in pleasing others.

In fact, proceeding in such a type of mission is like making a fool of oneself because the truth is that what to say of everybody, you can't satisfy even a single person on this earth fully. The reason being that everybody is a bundle of

73

countless expectations and desires and it is impossible to satisfy all the expectations of a person. **If there is anybody you can satisfy, it is only yourself and not anybody else**. In a similar way, any other person can be satisfied only by himself and not by anybody else.

Excess formalities which are so much prevalent in the Indian society are nothing but a part of artificially pleasing others. For example, let us take the case of a party in which a person is taking a glass of water from the designated place of drinking water by himself. Now if he is a V.I.P. whom you want to please, you will not allow him to take water himself. Similarly, you will not let him put his used glass to the designated place by himself. You will fight to do these jobs by yourself, although, there is nothing wrong if he does these jobs by himself in the party.

Spirituality highly discourages trying to please people artificially. So don't waste unnecessary time and energy in trying to please people and make them happy artificially. Trying always leads to undesirable results. Happiness is a natural and effortless state of mind. Happiness can't be given or transmitted to others by force. When your mind is calm and quiet and rid of all negative emotions, you automatically experience happiness. Happiness is not an object which can be given to somebody. It is a feeling which one has to experience within oneself. **The greatest contribution, you can make in making other people happy is that you first make yourself happy** so that the vibrations emitted by you induce a similar state in others.

In short, **you can simply share your own happiness with others. You can't bring it from somewhere else and secondly, it is a spontaneous transfer. You can't make anybody happy by trying or by force.** Happiness is a very delicate thing. As soon as you apply force, it gets destroyed. But in this world, we find that there are people who themselves are unhappy and miserable and are trying to make others happy. What a fun! Isn't it?

■■■

Freedom from Dependency

A person always feeling dependent on something or somebody can never be happy. Only an independent person can be happy. However, here the word 'independence' doesn't mean that you should develop an ego or pride that you are supreme in the world and you don't need anybody

> Please don't shift to the other house, I can't live without you.

Dependency on others causes misery

or anything for your survival, and that others are all inferior and dependent on you. In fact, taking and giving help to each other, whenever required doesn't come under the word 'dependence'. Helping each other freely whenever

75

required is our natural birthright and is totally a different thing than dependence.

What we mean by the word, 'Dependence' is that you shouldn't psychologically feel that you can't live without a particular person or a particular thing and you will feel helpless without it. Feeling of independence means that you can always live joyfully without depending on a particular person or a particular thing. You feel that whenever any help is needed, the Supreme (God) can choose any means to help you through any person or a thing or a situation. There is no emphasis on a particular person or a thing. Any person or a thing may come forward for your help. All are equally welcome.

Feeling independent means the realization that real help comes from 'God' only. Other persons or things simply become a passage or means to transmit that help to you. They are not the real helpers. In this sense, you should only see the inspiration of God in the help being provided by your relatives, friends or anybody. These persons only act as agents or messengers of God or the Almighty.

So finally, to become dependent only on God is the real independency.

■■■

Freedom from Attachment in Relationships

Why do we develop so much attachment in our relations and invest so much in relationships? There are possibly three reasons:

Excessive attachment in relations is not good for your overall growth.

1. You can't remain alone, you want some kind of a cover for your loneliness. So you gather a lot of people around you so that you never have the time to feel that you are alone.

2. You feel that relations will help you in times of need. You feel afraid that if they are not there to support you, you will be left helpless. So there is a sort of dependency on your relations.

3. You feel you have some persons around to share your achievements, your excitements and to show off your superiority.

But all the above reasons from the point of view of reality are false. This is because you must learn to live alone happily because relatives will not always be there beside you. Sometimes, you will go away from them and sometimes, they will go away from you. Sometimes, some will pass away from the world. Similarly, as I have told you in Chapter 27 (Freedom from Dependency) that real help is always done by God. Other people simply become the conduit or medium. They are not the real helpers. And the third point, above is nothing but your superiority complex and ego which is definitely not worth discussing.

According to spirituality, all your relations including your parents, brothers and sisters are given to you according to your *karmic* bondage with them so that you can settle your *karmas* with them. So relatives are not some special people whom you have to see differently from others. They are like any other people in the world but have been temporarily linked to your present life by the law of *karma*. It is also to be noted that although you have some choice in making friends but in matter of relatives, there is no choice. They are already karmically determined right from your birth. Even our marriage is also supposed to be karmically determined although outwardly it may appear to be our free choice. Even if one may think that he or she has chosen his or her partner by his or her free will but what about your in-laws and other relations on your partner's side which automatically get linked to you after your marriage on whom you have no control. So from this angle, your only job is to perform your duties selflessly which that relation calls for, exchange help when needed, show tolerance, patience and adjustment at the adverse behaviour of others but not get entangled in the game of expectations, comparison of give and take, etc. because it will increase the bondage of *karma* instead of dissolving it.

So in short, your obligation with your relatives is of simply fulfilling your duty but not of clinging and expecting something from them. Then only, you will be able to keep away from the bitterness which you see all around in relationships.

One easy way to loosen your attachment to your relatives is to strengthen attachment with God. **Once a higher attachment is developed, lower attachments automatically fall off**. What you are searching in your relatives/friends, is already available in God in much more abundance.

■■■

Freedom from Unreasonable Desires

Our religions often speak of desirelessness and as an ordinary person always thinks how a human being can be free from desires? It is the desires only which keep him active throughout the life. To a layman, the desireless person will look like a dead and dull person.

Arabpati

Karorpati

Lakhpati

Desires multiply faster than you can satisfy them.

But what our religious scriptures mean by the word 'desires' is the ego-based or negative desires which, although, keep you active but at the same time keep you restless, tense and in the end, reward you with dust and nothing valuable and worthwhile is achieved by you. In spite of all the running about, you remain empty handed in the end.

On the other hand, desire to grow or desire to improve your health, desire to know yourself, desire to know God, desire for the knowledge of life, desire to do something creative or constructive for the benefit of all, etc. are all beneficial desires. Similarly, there are certain basic needs for survival and for leading a comfortable life. We are also not preventing you from pursuing these. In fact, these basic needs don't come under the word 'desires'. **There are some foolish people in the world who torture their bodies by nonfulfilment of the basic needs and comforts of the body and claim that they have achieved freedom from worldly desires. Our title doesn't respect such ignorance and rather condemns such mindless actions.**

So coming back to our main theme, what are the ego-based desires which are to be eliminated gradually? They can be categorized as below:

1. Desire for name, fame, status, power, recognition, etc.

2. Desire for *Rajasik* pleasures (pleasures which keep you excited, e.g., seeing a sensational and violent movie, eating spicy and stimulating foods/drinks, reading sensational news, reading detective novels/ stories, etc.

3. Desire for amassing as much money, wealth and property, as possible, desire for making contacts with influential persons and people in power, etc. (These desires are basically because of the feeling of insecurity because your ego always feels insecure.)

The above desires keep you perpetually tense and excited. You run after them with the illusion that they will give you permanent satisfaction which never happens because **in the domain of excitement, the formula is, The more you get, the more you want.** So this becomes a trap.

The only right desire in life which will give you ever lasting joy is to continuously grow spiritually by raising the level of your consciousness more and more which finally culminates in **Self-realization.** Your inner Self is the source of permanent joy and satisfaction which you are actually seeking at the bottom of your heart. All the chapters in this book aim towards attainment of this goal only.

■■■

Freedom from Negative Emotions

There is no direct way to be free from negative emotions because negative emotions are simply the symptoms of a disease. They are not the disease itself. And if you start fighting with the symptoms instead of the disease, you know what will be the result. Negative emotions are simply the byproduct when you are working under your **Lower Nature**. Similarly, positive emotions are the byproduct of working under your **Higher Nature**.

Negative emotions ruin your body and mind.

To illustrate it further, suppose a person is highly selfish, egoistic, attached, etc., he can't avoid negative emotions creeping in himself. If you are advising such a person to leave his negative emotions (e.g. jealousy, hatred, impatience, anger, fear, restlessness, irritation, anxiety, depression, hurry, panic, excitement, etc.) without first overcoming his Lower Nature, you are asking for the impossible.

Similarly, suppose a person is established in Higher Nature (i.e. filled with qualities of humbleness, kindness, respectfulness, assertiveness, equanimity, balance and stability, truthfulness, honesty, faith, trust and other positive qualities), he will automatically exude positive emotions (i.e. peace, love, joy, bliss, optimism, hope, confidence, etc.) without any effort on his part.

Now how to overcome the Lower Nature and how to be established in your Higher Nature? This is a million dollar question and this is what Yoga and spirituality is all about. You should attend to various Yoga and spiritual practices like *Hatha Yoga, Raja Yoga* (or *Dhyan Yoga*), *Karma Yoga, Bhakti Yoga, Gyan Yoga*, etc. for developing your Higher Nature and subsiding your Lower Nature. In addition to these spiritual practices, one important way to develop your Higher Nature and to weaken your Lower Nature is **Meditation in Action** which is nothing but trying to remain conscious while doing any activity in practical life and never allow any activity to happen unconsciously without your awareness and mindfulness. This is because the Lower Nature gets a chance to erupt only when you are unconscious. Whenever you are conscious, your Higher Nature gets activated.

I may point out one thing here that there are certain emotions which are not all the time negative. For example, take the case of anger. If some real bad thing is occurring in front of your eyes, then feeling bad and little angry is natural. Only thing is that you have the power to control yourself so that this feeling of badness doesn't convert into uncontrolled outburst of anger. **You can transmute this feeling of anger into assertiveness and seriousness to control the bad situation.**

Similarly, take the case of fear. If some danger is there to your physical survival and existence, development of the feeling of fear is normal as a natural instinct. But again with the power of courage and presence of mind, you can control yourself and handle the situation boldly.

Similarly, take the case of the feeling of attachment. It is natural that anything which gives you some benefit, comfort or which you like, you are bound to develop some attachment towords it as a natural instinct. But again with the help of your intellect, discrimination and knowledge of the reality of life, you can realize that since all material things in this life are transient and impermanent, it is not worth developing undue emotional attachment to anything. Howsoever pleasant and useful a thing may be, but we should be emotionally able to let it go after our use and enjoyment.

Further take the case of the emotion of sadness and grief. If a genuine loss has occurred, for example, the death of a great man, then feeling sad and grieved is quite natural. But feeling sad over worthless things (for example when your new car has got a dent while driving) is wrong.

■■■

Note: For knowing more about the physiology and psychology of negative emotions, please read my books titled *'How to Control Anger'* and *'How to Overcome Fear'*.

Freedom from Strain of Perfectionism

There are many people in the world, who remain under strain because they expect perfectionism in everything from themselves and others and they are not able to get it. These

> I want perfect work from everybody and if anybody is not able to give it, he will be shunted out.

Adamancy for perfection only builds tension.

people lack the basic knowledge of the laws of life. We, human beings by our very definition are imperfect. Perfection is only attributed to 'God'. No matter at what level we reach, we can't avoid making mistakes. We can reduce our imperfections by constant knowledge and practice but we can never achieve complete perfection. *(A human being achieves perfection only when he attains the highest state of consciousness which is called 'moksha' or 'nirvana' or 'mukti' or 'God Realisation'. At this stage, he doesn't remain an ordinary human being and becomes the co-partner of God. He needn't further return to this earth for learning more lessons or attaining more perfection and is freed from the cycle of birth and death.)*

There are some persons who insist on getting one single perfect solution of a problem. What is needed is that instead of stressing upon one single perfect solution of any problem, one should strive to get an adequate number of reasonable solutions which, for our practical purposes, will be good enough to execute. **Expecting only perfectionism and idealism in every situation will constantly lead to stress**.

Committing mistakes or showing imperfectionism is quite natural for human beings. There is nothing unusual or criminal in it. There is no need to hide yourself or feel ashamed or guilty after committing mistakes. Important thing is to learn necessary lessons from the mistakes and constantly improve yourself from A to B, B to C, C to D and so on. Don't remain stuck in your life's journey at one point. You have to improve constantly every moment and in every sphere of life. **If we don't learn from our mistakes, we lose the benefit of the lesson which every mistake brings with it**.

■■■

Freedom from Hypocrisy

'Hypocrisy' means you have one thing inside you but you are showing a different thing from outside. Your inside and outside don't match. In other words, you have got two faces. One is real which you are hiding and the other is false which you are showing to others. You can realize the tremendous strain in which a person of this type has to live or survive.

Trying to show double faces is the biggest source of stress.

Now, why a person becomes a hypocrite. There may be various reasons like impressing and pleasing others, fear of rejection, dishonour, disapproval from others, etc. A spiritual person is characterised by a transparent inner and outer face without any difference whether it impresses other persons or not. **In fact, the acid test of a righteous person is that his thoughts, words and deeds should show resemblance with each other.**

Why is hypocrisy bad? Because it doesn't allow you to be natural or to be yourself. You have to be all the time under tremendous strain and stress to show off to others what you are not. To be artificial involves a lot of stress while to be natural, no effort or no stress is required. Gradually, hypocrisy makes you a split personality, i.e., two in one. I still remember the beautiful quote by a person which goes like this, **"Nothing is as stressful as trying to pretend to be what you are not"**.

Now, the way to leave hypocrisy is that don't bother to show off or impress others unnecessarily. Rather, work from the point of view of self-satisfaction, i.e., do what satisfies you, makes you feel good, comfortable and at ease.

■■■

Freedom from Suppression

In layman's terminology, 'suppression' means that you want to do a certain thing but are not able to do that due to a certain reason; then you suppress that thing inside your mind. The desire to do that thing still remains but you push the thing **from the conscious to the subconscious mind.**

Constant suppression of your feelings leads to explosion, one day.

Lot of conflicting things have been said about this word. Some theories say that you shouldn't suppress anything. Whatever comes to your mind, you should say or do that, so that you are relieved and no suffocation or pressure remains inside. Another theory says that if we give a free hand to people to do or say what comes in their mind, then law and order will break and there will be a lot of chaos and relationship problems.

We have to find a solution from the right perspective. We have to appreciate the following facts with regard to suppression.

1. There is not need to suppress a thing which is right. It can be freely expressed. If you suppress it, it will harm your psyche and may try to come out from other channels in a perverted form.

2. A thing which is wrong should be eliminated from your mind by the right understanding and needn't be suppressed.

A wrong thing can't be eliminated by hiding and suppression. By suppression, it becomes more powerful and continuously disturbs you from within. To eliminate a wrong thing, you have to first see it in all its nudity, then to consciously observe it, analyze it and examine it as to how it is coming, why it is coming, from where it is coming and what harm it is doing to you?

Thereafter, on the basis of this understanding, you control it. Then it won't become a suppression. Rather, it increases your will power and mental strength. **Suppression occurs when you control a thing out of compulsion because of some outside forces (like fear, temptation, maintaining your image in the eyes of others) and not by your own understanding**.

I will illustrate suppression by taking an example. A lot has been said in our society and culture regarding the control of sex. In many of our old religious scriptures, emphasis has been laid on abstinence from sex and virtue of 'Brahmacharya' or Celibacy. Now let us examine this issue in terms of facts, earlier stated.

Sex is a normal biological urge installed in our body by nature. There is full fledged sexual system in our body (sex glands, sex hormones, sex centre in brain, etc.) which governs the arousal and satisfaction of this urge. So sexual urge can't be wrong and abnormal. Now, if it is right and natural, then there is no question of suppression of this urge. It can be and should be expressed for the normal health of the body. Suppression of a natural thing can create various problems in the body and mind. Now the only thing is that even for a right and natural thing, there are healthy and unhealthy ways of fulfillment of an urge. For example, hunger is a basic urge but you can satisfy this urge both in a healthy way (eating wholesome foods in the right quantity and at the right time) or in an unhealthy way (eating junk foods in abnormal quantity and at irregular intervals). So is with sex. Sex with a prostitute, call girl, forcible sex (e.g. rape, molestation, eve teasing, homosexuality, sex with animals, over indulgence in sex, sex with multiple partners, etc. are examples of unhealthy sex). While sex with one clean partner, done with mutual agreement (i.e., not by force) and in a controlled and limited way as per the normal capacity of the body is an example of healthy sex. Please note that God has given human beings a faculty of 'control' by which he can control his expressions of natural urges also to some extent if the situation demands without any harm to him. It is only the excessive control or suppression of an urge which harms the entire system.

■■■

Freedom from Longing for Name, Fame and Power

Our ego's greatest desire or ambition in life is to earn name, fame, recognition, status and power (domination and control over others). Ego always wants to remain high or great in the eyes of others. It wants that the maximum number of people should know him or her. Not only this, it

My dear son, I want you to earn a big name, fame & power when you grow up.

Parents themselves prompt the children to entangle in the rat race of name, fame & recognition.

also wants to have power and control over others. Our ego feels elevated when it can manipulate others as it likes.

But this desire itself is the greatest cause of stress, frustration and perpetual anxiety for the ego for the following simple reasons:

1. Firstly, it is not easy to achieve what our ego is desiring because there are umpteen number of competitors who are also desiring the same. This non-fulfillment or partial fulfillment of the desire keeps the ego in an ever tense and turbulent state.

2. This world is relative by its very structure. No matter how much name, fame and power you have, there will be always some people who will be ahead of you. Similarly, there will be some persons who are below you today, but tomorrow, they may rise above you. So everything is relative in this realm. But your ambition is to come to the top and not to remain behind anybody. That is what keeps you in perpetual frustration and disappointment.

3. Thirdly, getting name, fame and power is only one side of the picture. The world is dual in its nature. The other side of the picture is that once you get more name, fame, position and power, then you come in the limelight and become more exposed to both good and bad elements. In the position of power, your responsibilities also increase. Many times, you have to take decisions which are not favourable and pleasant to everybody and which increase the number of your critics and enemies who are always on the lookout to trap you somewhere or the other by searching some loophole or weakness on your side. Further, at high positions, your security and safety is also a bit endangered. You can't move about that freely.

So although, outwardly, it may look very enchanting that so many people know you, bow before you, flatter you; media frequently quotes your name; newspapers and magazines keep you in the list of celebrities, but the price you pay for all this is much higher and not worth it.

That is why, a spiritual person never hankers after name, fame, power and recognition. Rather, he dislikes the same.

If they come to him spontaneously as a byproduct of his qualities and work, it is all right, but they are never his goal. He is only immersed in the joy of the inner Self which has no negatives and risks associated with it and is always available with you in abundance without any fear of it being taken away by somebody else.

■■■

Freedom from Possessiveness of Human Beings

The word, 'possessiveness' is used when we try to possess human beings like objects. As soon as we possess a human being, we insult him heavily because we convert him into an inanimate object. Only objects can be possessed not living beings.

> You can't go anywhere without my permission.

Possessiveness destroys the beauty of a relationship.

Living beings have soul, feelings and a dignity. They can't be treated and manipulated like objects. But what we see in the practical life that a person is treating his servants and subordinates just like things without bothering that they have feelings, emotions and a heart. He treats them like lifeless machines. Whenever there is exploitation, slavery, torture, use of force and insult to human beings, it is an indication that they are being treated like things and machines.

Human beings must be treated differently from the lifeless objects. They should be dealt with respect and dignity just like yourself. You can request them, advise them but never force them, order them or manipulate them. We inflict a great damage to the soul when it is treated with disrespect and is used as an object for selfish ends by somebody.

Possessiveness can be understood best by giving a popular example. Suppose, there is a bird freely and cheerfully flying in the sky. Now you catch it and put it in a cage. You will find that all its cheerfulness, charm and beauty has gone away and it is almost dead like a corpse though it is the same bird. In the same way, when we possess a human being, it is almost like suffocating him, not allowing him to breathe and grow.

Sometimes, we show this attitude of possessiveness towards our partners (husband/wife), towards our children or other family relations and hide it in the name of 'love'. In the name of 'love', most of the time, we crush and destroy the other person. Can we call it real love? Does any person have the right to be so possessive of another human being?

■■■

Freedom from Over-occupation

You may have seen many people in your lives who are working like a donkey from morning to night. They are involved in many types of businesses and in many deals apart from their regular jobs. Even if some free time is available, they will immediately rush to some movie, market, or some eating place but they will not let themselves be relaxed, unoccupied or free for sometime.

Some persons remain overbusy in useless things throughout their lives.

If they are forced to sit some day without any work or anything to do, they feel like dying, utterly empty and bored. Why is it so? Because they have not yet tasted the inner joy and peace of their inner Self. A person who has learned to turn his attention inwards and taste this inner joy will rather welcome those moments when he can sit relaxed, unoccupied for sometime so that he can remain immersed in his inner Self and become rejuvenated and fresh.

The person who is unacquainted with this joy has no option but to keep his mind busy, distracted somewhere or the other, so that he doesn't feel empty or bored. A person who remains constantly busy and his activity is not balanced by relaxation, creates an imbalance in his body and mind which proves detrimental to him in the long run. **For a balance, relaxation and activity should constantly alternate. They should be in a dynamic balance with each other**.

The only way to remove this imbalance is to learn to sit quietly without any work for sometime in a day. During this time, you can focus on your incoming and outgoing breath at your nose tip or abdomen. This practice will calm your mind within a few minutes. Once your mind calms and becomes still, it starts turning inwards and gradually, starts having the glimpses of the joy and peace of your inner Self. Once this contact is made, then it works like a magnet and you are gradually pulled towards your **Centre (inner Self)**, slowly and slowly.

Initially, you may find it very difficult to sit quiet and focus on your breath for a longer time because your mind will pull you out again and again outwards. But with sustained practice and will-power, you will gradually be able to sit calmly for a longer time and begin to cherish these moments which is a good sign for your progress. Further, when you turn inwards, initially, you will see only darkness and the various *samskaras* deposited in your subconscious mind will gradually come out and disappear as you watch them. **With the thinning and disappearing of your *samskaras*, you will start seeing the light of your inner Self, gradually**. The ability to sit unoccupied and do nothing, at least for sometime in a day is a good practice and will pay you greatly in life.

■■■

Freedom from Over-involvement in Worldly Affairs

If you look around, you will find that people are mindlessly involved in innumerable things, whether it is actually needed or not. Whatever things come to their attention,

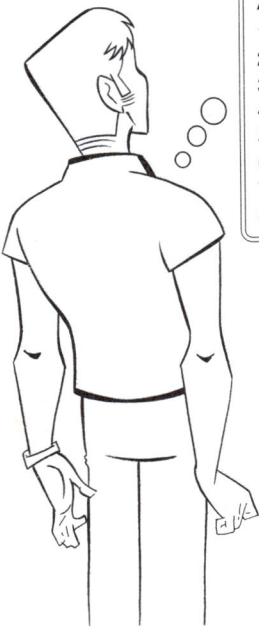

Agenda for the day:
1. Movie
2. Birthday party
3. Receive friend at Railway Station.
4. Seeing off a relative to airport
5. New year Celebration
6. T.V. Serial
7. Newspaper, Magazines
8. Cybercafe.

We remain mindlessly involved in various worldly affairs without stopping for a single minute.

their minds get entrapped in it. One of the greatest requirements for happiness is to be selective and choosy in

99

life in what you see, hear, read, do, and not to do anything and everything mindlessly.

The world is a big jungle. The more you enter into it, the more you are lost and confused. Hence, involve yourself in the worldly matters only to the extent which is required for your survival, growth and carrying out your worldly duties. Avoid unnecessary involvements here and there, roaming here and there, peeping and poking your nose here and there in others affairs and scandals (which are always available in plenty). Unnecessary and extra involvement in worldly affairs create distractions in mind and senses which is not conducive to your mental peace and spiritual development.

Similarly, reduce your collection of worldly possessions and luxuries to the bare minimum which are just necessary for your survival and are the basic comforts of life. Normally, it is observed that we collect much more than our requirements. The tendency to hoard and collect more and more things, whether you require them or not, eventually brings more and more anxieties, tensions and dissipation of your energy in ensuring their security, regular maintenance and unnecessary blockage of space and money by them.

■■■

Freedom from Attention on Others

This is the basic characteristic of our ego that it always keeps it's attention on others. It is more interested in what others are doing, what others have bought, what others possess, who has come in the neighbour's house, who is having an affair with whom, which husbands and wives have strained relations, which housewife is having bitter relations with her mother-in-law, which relative's son has failed in a competitive examination, so on and so forth.

Where is my neighbour going in the early morning. There is something fishy.

Most of the times our attention remains on others rather than on ourselves.

It never occurs to our ego to put its attention on itself and analyse what it is doing and what is its aim? On the other hand, a spiritual person or a person devoid of ego and centred in his Self keeps his attention on himself and doesn't bother about others. This is the basic difference between the two types of persons. Ego not only bothers about others, but it also goes further ahead in poking its nose in others' business, interfering in their activities, making comments/ remarks about others, giving advice to others, whether asked or not.

Now, our ego has to pay a heavy price for this habit. Firstly, nobody likes interfering and poking of nose by others in their affairs. So such a person is disliked and avoided by everybody. Secondly, your own progress is halted because your attention is on others and not on yourself. Thirdly, you remain all the time anxious, curious and not relaxed because if you want to keep your current affairs about others up-to-date, you have to remain in this state of mind.

Hence, concentrate only on your progress in life. Don't waste time in bothering and interfering in what others are doing. Also avoid making remarks and comments about others because you are still not fit to do that. Only a person who has achieved perfection is fit to make a remark or comment upon others.

You should also avoid the habit of giving unnecessary advice to anyone, when not asked. You should give advice only when asked for and if you are not knowledgeable in that matter, apologize instead of giving a wrong or a vague advice. In fact, even if you really want to give any useful advice on your own for the benefit of others, it is better to impart this from your behaviour rather than from your words. Then it will have more weightage and value.

■■■

Freedom from Self Centredness

There are some people whose whole life is filled with 'I', 'me', 'mine', etc. Their conversation always goes like this, "I was this", "I had done this", "I like this" and so on. It appears from their talks that they constitute the whole world and there is nothing else in the world except them.

> I was the chairman of that high level committee. I was the mastermind behind that building project.

A self-centered person is characterized by lot of 'I', 'me' and 'mine' in his talks.

In fact, talking and thinking only of ourselves is a sign of very narrow and low level of consciousness by which we make ourselves very small. We no longer remain a part of this universe and a participant in the great *'leela'* of God.

We become separated and therefore, feel loneliness, discomfort and disharmony with the rest of the universe.

Consider yourself a part of this universe and a part of the grand 'leela' of God which is unfolding here. You are not separate from other persons and this universe. We may apparently feel that all human beings are separate from each other, but the fact is that this separation is only physical. Mentally, we are all connected to each other. That is why, we sense each other's pleasures and pains. Each mind is connected with every other mind and all the minds in turn are connected with the cosmic mind (God). So there is a great interrelationship between everybody. No human is an iceland in himself. Everybody's activity makes a ripple in the whole universe howsoever infinitesimal it may be. In fact, each mind is in communion with the whole universe.

All of us have common needs and goals and all of us bear the same relationship with God. Thinking and doing various works from the consideration of common benefit and from a universal vision is a sign of expanded consciousness and it truly fulfils our mission and goal on this earth. Doing everything from the view point of only personal gain is highly selfish and unbecoming of us as a human being. This negates the very purpose of our existence in this world. **Exercise your will power to stop yourself whenever you are tempted to boast about yourself or to talk only about your own interests or problems**. In fact, when the consciousness is enlarged, the idea of living and working solely for oneself appears quite absurd.

Your concern for well being shouldn't be confined to you or your near and dear ones. It should encompass the whole world in it. If you see or hear someone suffering anywhere, it should bring in your heart the same sympathy and concern as when you suffer yourself, i.e., you should be able to look upon others' problems as your own problems by placing yourself mentally in their position. We should have a clear realization that whatever comforts and luxuries we require, others also require the same, and by whatever things we feel discomfort, pain, etc., others also feel in the same way by those things. When we actually realize the above fact, then our consciousness truly expands to the concept of a **Global family**. In this state, our relationship with everybody in the world becomes the same and nobody remains close or far.

Hence, leave the attitude of doing everything only for your own comforts, pleasures and profits. You should strive and work from the point of view that everybody is going to be comfortable and better and not only yourself. Your effort should be directed like this. For example, suppose, you don't have heaters in your office for the winter season. One way is to think that let me have a heater for my room so that at least, I will be comfortable. This is a selfish attitude. Another angle of thinking is that we should make such arrangements that all the persons may remain in comfort. This is a broader attitude by which the whole world will benefit.

In short, we should always remember the maxim. **In the well being of all, lies our own well being. If our neighbour is crying, we can't remain comfortable in spite of all luxuries**.

Freedom from Jealousy

What is jealousy and how is it produced? Jealousy occurs when we find some person in our acquaintance, e.g., in office, neighbourhood, relations, etc. going higher or becoming better than us in any respect. As soon as somebody becomes superior to us or we feel so, jealousy begins. We can't tolerate that anybody should be superior to us. Then we start justifying our feelings of jealousy by criticizing that the person has reached to that position by unfair means or by some political pull or somebody's influence.

How has he bought such a costly car in such a short time? He must be a corrupt man.

As soon as we see somebody having a better thing than us, we become filled with jealously instead of joy.

It is the basic problem with our ego that it always wants to remain superior in comparison to others. Whenever this desire gets defeated, our ego feels hurt and jealous. Suppose, you have a beautiful house to live in but your neighbour builds a better house than yours, jealousy begins. You may have a grand car but if your neighbour or a colleague or a relative buys a more expensive and superior car, your peace is disturbed although you still have the same car which was giving you so much joy till now.

Hence, you can see that the **basis of jealousy is comparison**. If you don't compare and don't give unnecessary attention to others and enjoy what you have, there is no question of jealousy. This is what spirituality teaches us that try to find joy and satisfaction from what you have. **If you lack in something, try to improve yourself but do not compare with others. Don't try to live a life of comparison**. Live solely according to your independent needs and comforts. Another thing with regard to comparison is that there is no end to it. Even if you are able to raise yourself to the level of the person, whom you are jealous of, still there is no guarantee that in future, he will not again rise above you. What will you do then?

Secondly, you may rise above one person by making efforts. But what about others?

So the best way to say goodbye to jealousy is to put an end to the habit of comparison.

Once comparison is gone, you have removed the very root of jealousy. In fact, as you develop spiritually, you will find that the progress and well being of others creates happiness in your mind, rather than jealousy. This is the true sign of overcoming jealousy.

■■■

Freedom from Over-accumulation of Material Knowledge & Information

Knowledge of worldly matters is unlimited. It is not practically possible to have a perfect knowledge of everything by any person. So it is better to be an expert only in one line and serve the world in that area rather than trying to gain knowledge of everything. In other areas, you can simply possess a general knowledge for the purpose of survival and worldly interactions. There are people who want to gain maximum knowledge in all the fields. They end up becoming mad because neither it is practically possible nor it is necessary and desirable.

DICTIONARY
PHYSICS
GENERAL KNOWLEDGE

*Over accumulation of unwanted knowledge,
information, etc. simply creates stress.*

Similarly, some people have the habit of accumulating unnecessary information. For example, suppose you are collecting an information of names of all the railway stations of India, names of various trains passing through different stations, their timings, the distance between one station to another, etc. Is there any use of spending time in collecting this information? Only a limited information is useful when you are travelling from one particular station to another. Hence, collect only that much information which is necessary for your day-to-day survival and dealings and it is not wise to waste your time, energy and brain in collecting information which is not practically useful for you. In this world, you are constantly bombarded by a massive amount of information and data all the time and from various areas. **If you become involved in collecting all the information, even for the sake of interest, you will go mad. So be very selective in choosing as to what is really needed by you and spend your time only in that.**

Our final aim is the knowledge of the Self which will only liberate us from all sufferings and miseries. Worldly knowledge can't give you that final freedom or bliss which you are looking for. **Worldly knowledge is only a means to our better survival in the world. Attainment of more and more worldly knowledge is not our goal.** Our ultimate goal is the knowledge of life as to who am I? What is the real purpose of this life? Who is God? What is my relationship with the Cosmos? What is my relationship with God? What is the purpose of this universe?

Contemplation on these essential questions will give you the glimpse of the meaning and purpose of your existence.

■■■

Freedom from Craving for Other's Attention

Trying to attract other's attention on us implies that we want to remain high in the opinion of others whether we are actually so or not. We can't stand a low rating of ourselves by others. We fail to recognise the tremendous strain we are putting on ourselves in this process.

Many persons try to become glamourous
to attract other's attention in a gathering.

By trying to impress others and thereby getting joy, you are indirectly giving the key of your happiness to others. That is, if they want, they will make you happy and if they want, they can make your life miserable. You simply become a puppet in the hands of others who will make you dance to the tune they like. In other words, you reduce yourself to a slave or a beggar by mortgaging your happiness on the mercy of others.

Your happiness and contentment should rest in yourself and you should do any work primarily from the point of view of your own satisfaction. You should derive the joy right from your attitude towards what you are doing. Your joy shouldn't wait for the time when somebody will come and appreciate your work.

Don't give much weightage to other people whether they know your calibre or capabilities or whether they overestimate or underestimate you. There are many people in the world who don't know at all about you. Is it making any difference to you? **Your estimation in your own eyes is more important**. Other people's comments should be taken only objectively as an opportunity to re-examine yourself and take any corrective action if required. Even if you find that you are weak in certain areas, it shouldn't matter much. In this diverse world, differences in the people are bound to be there. There is nothing unusual in it. In some areas, you may be better and in some areas, others may excel. To have a desire that you should be at the top in the world in all the areas and only you should be appreciated the most, is highly immature.

■■■

Freedom from the Results of Actions

Many people do work in this world with the sole aim of getting the desired results which they have already fixed in their minds before starting the work. Such people are never able to enjoy during the duration of their work because their eyes are always on the results and they are always worried whether they will get the desired results or not. Although they work tirelessly like a donkey, they remain constantly anxious and tense about the results due to which their efficiency and output also decreases compared to the input they give to the work.

Karma Yoga comes to our rescue in this situation and enlightens us about the right way of doing *Karma*. The *Karma Yoga* teaches us to enjoy right in the *Karma* or work by doing it with full interest, attention and awareness and

Learn to derive joy right from the work rather than from the results.

never bother about the results. It is a divine law that anything which you do with full attention and awareness becomes supremely interesting and joyful. Further, when you do a work (*Karma*) with full attention and awareness, the quality of the work or the output automatically improves which gives you the added joy.

As I have mentioned elsewhere that in spite of our best efforts, the results are not in our hands. So there is no point in dissipating our energy by constantly ruminating on the results. Further, this is also an illusion that after getting the desirable results, you will become happy forever. Even if you get very good results, it will only give you temporary excitement for a day, two days or three days. **The excitement can't last forever by its very nature**.

You can experience it yourself by an example. Suppose, you have stood first in any Board Examination. For how many days, can you remain excited? It will be a short affair of say, one or two weeks when your friends/relatives will be congratulating you on phone or in person; newspapers may be publishing your photo; press men or media persons may be coming to you for interviews. But this can't go on forever. Excitement in you and others will gradually fade and you will have to eventually come down to the earth.

So remember that the long lasting joy is only during the execution of the work. **Results only give temporary excitement but not the real joy and happiness**. Once, you are not attached to the results of your '*Karma*', you are also free from the bondage of *karma* which our 'religious scriptures' talk about. And once, you are free from the bondage of *karma*, you are free from the cycle of birth and death also because rebirth and reincarnation occurs because of the continuation of the effects of past *karmas*. If we are not attached to the *karma* or our work and don't carry its traces further in our minds, then the chain of the cause and effect is broken and the momentum of *karma* is lost to carry on further.

■■■

Freedom from Addictions and Intoxications

A considerable number of people, now a days, take some kind of addiction in the form of intoxicating and narcotic drugs. The purpose of these intoxications can be one of the following:

Mind altering drugs do more harm than good, in the long run.

1. To provide you stimulation – e.g., drugs like Amphetamines (even tea, coffee, cold drinks and smoking also provide you stimulation)

2. To make you drowsy, sleepy – e.g. drugs like Barbiturates (Tranquilizers like Calmpose, Valium, Alprax, etc. also do the same to some extent).

3. To make you forgetful of yourself – like alcohol. That's why by taking alcohol, you start behaving bizarre and without inhibitions.

4. To make you euphoric and see hallucinations – like L.S.D., Brown Sugar, etc.

If you analyze why people take these addictions, it clearly shows that these people are not able to get something naturally which they are trying to make up from these addictive substances. Let us show it with some examples. You try to get 'high' by taking some chemicals and drugs. There are natural ways also, for example, dancing, music, singing, aerobic exercises (e.g. swimming, running, walking, cycling, jumping exercises, etc.) which also give you a 'high' feeling. So why not try getting arousal from these natural methods which don't have any harmful side effects on the body and don't cause addiction also? With the artificial drugs, another problem is that very soon, you develop tolerance for the quantity of drug you are taking and then you have to continuously increase the quantity to give you the same stimulation. So it becomes a never ending chain.

Similarly, if you want to relax, there are better alternatives available in *Yoga* and nature cure, e.g. various stretching exercises (which relax your muscles), *yognidra*, passive awareness on some object, listening to soft/soothing music, listening to *bhajans* and devotional songs, chanting *mantras*, *pranayamas* (breathing exercises) cold water bath, various meditation techniques, etc. These are natural tranquilizers without any side effects.

Further, read good spiritual books which give you knowledge about the reality and truths of life. Once you have the real knowledge about a thing, you never become tense, confused, disillusioned and are able to face any problem with courage and right understanding. Therefore, you don't require any intoxicant to forget yourself or to hallucinate yourself in the face of adversities.

■■■

Freedom from Dishonesty, Cheating and Untruthfulness

This is a common statement today from many persons that now a days only dishonest, corrupt, liars and cheaters are flourishing and the honest and truthful people are suffering.

Before you cheat others, you have to cheat yourself.

But this is a very superficial statement and comes from an immature and undeveloped mind which doesn't realize the agony, which a dishonest and a cheater suffers

116

continuously from inside. **From outward glamour and show, you can't find out the inner state of a person's mind. It may be completely the reverse. That is to say, that a person may be in utmost peacelessness and tension from inside while on the outside, he may be flooded with wealth and richness**.

Please note that a dishonest and corrupt person can never be happy by the very divine laws of life since he is not aligned with his real Self. Anything contradictory to your real nature is bound to give you uneasiness and tension.

An honest person may have less money but he will be very peaceful, joyful and satisfied from inside (provided his honesty is not due to any outward compulsion or force). He will not like to kill his soul just for the sake of some money because the soul is much more precious than money. A dishonest person is engaged in the mad race after money just because he hasn't experienced the joy of the inner Self. A person who has experienced this joy can never be dishonest, untruthful and can't cheat anybody.

If you can peep inside the mind of a dishonest and corrupt person, you will find it filled with fears/anxieties (of getting caught, or getting exposed), guilt (of cheating, exploiting and blackmailing others), greed (how to get more and more money), stress (how and where to store the wealth so as to avoid legal and other complications), etc. Can such a person filled with these negative emotions enjoy life? It is also to be noted that whenever you harm somebody by dishonesty, cheating, telling lies, etc., the first and major harm is done to you. The harm done to the other person is only secondary, because the harm done to the other person is only in terms of money but the harm done to yourself is the harm caused to your soul which can't be easily settled and nullified.

■■■

Freedom from Guilt

'Guilt' is one word which has been grossly misused by the so called keepers of religion to exploit and blackmail simple and innocent people and keep them in perpetual fear and in a state of self condemnation or self hatred.

Father, I am guilty of staring at a girl Please pardon my sin so that I may not suffer in hell.

Creating guilt in a person is not the right way to mend him.

Once you tell somebody that you have done a very bad *karma* and God, in heaven, is very angry with you and you will have to burn in the eternal fire of hell after death, the person is half dead and will remain at your feet so that suggest some way for the reversal of his bad deed. Then you suggest some penance for him to reverse the effect of his bad deed like cleaning shoes in a temple for one month or donating a certain sum of money to a temple regularly.

This is how the so called keepers of religion (*Pundits, Padris, Mullahs,* etc.) get power over the innocent persons and such persons become their slaves with their souls almost dead. Unless you create guilt and fear in the person, he will not surrender before you and you will not have the power over him. This is the whole game of producing guilt in a person.

Please note that remaining always in guilt is not the desirable feature if you want to grow spiritually. We, human beings, are bound to make many mistakes and do many evil deeds till we attain the highest state of enlightenment. There is nothing to feel guilty about it. Instead of feeling constant by guilty over our bad actions, we should learn the necessary lessons from them and try not to repeat them for our own happiness in life.

Also note that there is no such angry God sitting in heaven waiting to take revenge or punish you for your bad deeds. God is always merciful and compassionate and is not pleased or annoyed by your good or bad deeds.

Your bad actions directly punish you by creating unease and tension in your mind. They can't be erased by doing any kind of penance or repentence. They can only be erased by changing those bad actions into good ones in future by realizing your mistake. If you don't change them, you will continue to suffer by the very law which says that bad deeds or wrong actions create tensions and pain in the mind.

A religious organization, a cult leader or a *guru* who controls his members by inflicting fear and guilt in them is doing a great disservice to his followers. Threatening the followers to burn in hell or fire for their wrong deeds is an erroneous message to manipulate them and is not a reality.

■■■

How to Remain Ever Free

47

Freedom from Group or Crowd

If you observe the psychology of people around, you will find that there is a strong tendency to attach to a certain organization, to a certain group or to a certain party and then follow the psychology of the mob which constitutes that organization.

In a crowd, you are carried away by the mob psychology and not by personal rational thinking.

Once you start following the dictates or rules of a group blindly, you lose your soul. You no more remain an individual. Spiritual upliftment and attainment of truth and happiness are totally personal things. A crowd can't attain happiness and *Moksha*. Only an individual can. Even when hundred people are doing meditation together, initially, they may start as a crowd but as soon as they turn inside, they are absolutely alone. **At your innermost core which is filled with joy and bliss, you are absolutely alone.**

120

We attach to the crowd because then we don't have to think and decide what is to be done. The crowd decides and we just follow the crowd. Similarly, we are not individually responsible also for what the crowd does. The whole crowd is responsible. So we feel a sort of security in belonging to a large group or crowd.

But with this, we also lose our individuality and the inner joy and happiness which follows an independent personality. In your practical life also, you have seen that only the weak travel in crowd (like a sheep always travels in a herd) and the strong and fearless always travel alone (like a lion).

What we mean to say is that if you really want to relish the juice of life, you will have to learn to become an individual and not strongly attach to a group, party, society, association or union and following their percepts blindly keeping your soul aside. Once you belong to a party, the party politics takes the upper hand which is an hindrance to your inner journey and spiritual development.

■■■

Freedom from Extremes

Our Lower Nature is like a pendulum which moves from one extreme of negative emotion to the another extreme. On the other hand, our Higher Nature remains stabilised in the middle. Its emotions (positive emotions) don't have extremes.

If you can describe two extremes of a pendulum as hot and cold, then the middle point can be described as cool (neither hot nor cold).

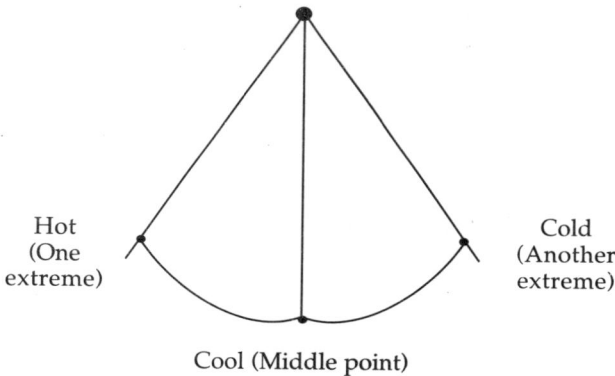

Hot
(One
extreme)

Cold
(Another
extreme)

Cool (Middle point)

Our ego moves from one extreme to another like a pendulum. It never rests in the middle.

A spiritual person established in Higher Nature is cool, i.e., at the middle point, while a material or a worldly person established in Lower Nature is either hot or cold but never cool.

For example, a person established in Lower Nature will get very excited (one extreme of the pendulum) if he gets some desired thing (like promotion, selection in a competition, etc.) and will get depressed (another extreme of the pendulum) if he doesn't get the desired thing. Taking another illustration, if someone or something is in favour of him, he will get highly attached to him ('*Raga*' in spiritual terminology) and if someone is against him, he will develop hatred for him ('*Dvesha*' in spiritual terminology). Both are extremes.

Take one more example. If a person develops feelings of superiority complex over some attainment, he will also easily develop the feeling of inferiority complex when he fails to achieve something in comparison to others. Both are extreme conditions. On the other hand, a spiritual person established in Higher Nature neither gets excited in some achievement nor gets depressed in failures. Similarly, he neither develops *Raga* for those who are in his favour nor hatred or *Dvesha* for those who are against him. He remains neutral and stable at the middle point. Similarly, a spiritual person neither has feelings of superiority complex nor of inferiority complex over any achievement. He simply remains self confident in whatever he does without any comparison with others. This is also called the stage of equanimity.

This is to be remembered that **if you are at one extreme, you are bound to go to the another extreme after sometime. You can't remain at one extreme permanently. Extremes are points of unrest or instability. For example, if a person has *raga* (or attachment) with something or some person, he is bound to have *dvesha* (hatred) with some other thing or person.**

The central purpose of spirituality and Yoga is to bring the person from the extremes to the middle point. Till you live in extremes, you are never at ease but always restless and agitated. The various practices of Yoga and change in mental attitudes as explained in various chapters will help you to come to the middle point, i.e., to the point of rest.

■■■

Freedom from Rejections and Disapprovals by Others

There are many people who give more importance to what people think about them than what they think about themselves. They get very upset when they or their works or their views are rejected and disapproved by somebody. They start feeling that they are worthless and inferior compared to other people and consequently, develop depression and hopelessness.

We shouldn't get influenced by other's rejection.

If you do so, you are making a very false assumption that the person rejecting you is always right and you are always wrong. The person rejecting you may not be technically

124

competent for evaluating you or he may be biased and jealous of you. So how can you take him to be correct? **Only an enlightened person who has remained very close to you, can give a correct judgement about you.**

Hence, you should always take the comments of the other person about you as simply a matter of his opinion and that opinion may not be correct or may be only partially correct. In fact, when a person gives his opinion about you or your works, it tells more about his mental make up and attitude rather than yours.

So, instead of getting carried away by the opinion and judgements of others, you should, at such an occasion, stop for a while and reexamine yourself. If you feel that there is certainly a scope for improvement on that account, then take corrective measures. If you feel that there is no weight in the comments of the other person, just ignore them instead of giving them more weightage by constant thinking.

Please note that it is more important for you as to what you think about yourself than what others think about you. Your self analysis about you is more important. Don't get carried away by the judgement/opinion of others about you whether it be your praise or criticism. Weigh them with your intellect and accept only those which you consider appropriate.

■■■

Freedom from Overthinking

Some people waste a lot of their time in thinking, planning and imagining things. They continuously remain in a dream world imagining that they want to do this and that. Although their intentions are not bad and they really want

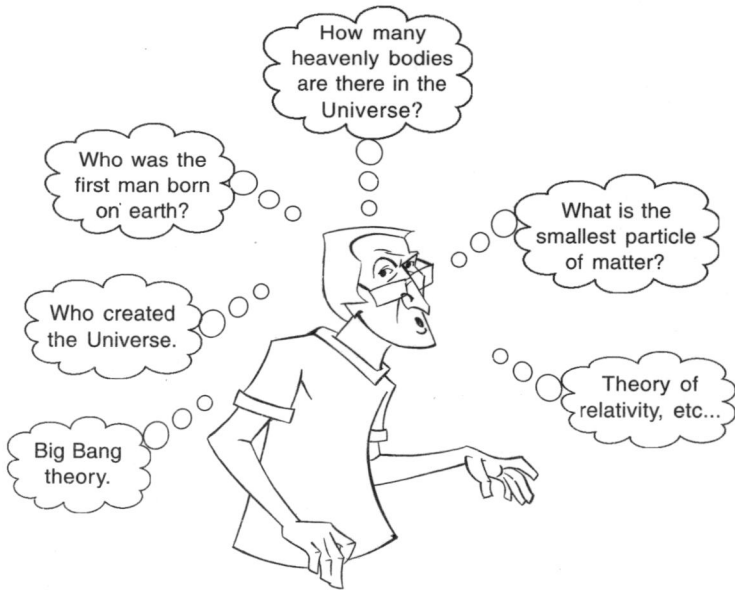

Overthinking leads to confusion and chaos in the mind.

to learn and achieve much in life but they are not able to achieve what they really want because their approach is not correct. This is because most of their time is lost in thinking and imaging things. Even when they actually work, their mind remains on their future plans only. So they are not able to do their present work properly which results in further frustration and depression.

Although certain amount of thinking and planning is very necessary for doing a job well, it is the over thinking and planning which is bad. The best way to stop this constant mental chatter and achieve maximum in life is that never allow yourself idling and day dreaming for a long time. Always take up something constructive (from your big list of works) and get absorbed in it. Then take up another and get absorbed in it. **Your frustration comes from the fact that you want to do, learn and achieve everything just now or in the least possible time**. This as you know is practically impossible. Moreover, you also know that your desires and plans also keep on changing as a function of time. For example, your desires and plans are not the same as you had twenty years ago. At that time (twenty years ago), you were so desperate about certain things but now you are not. The practical approach is that you make a list of whatever you want to do, go on adding in that list as new ideas come up in your mind but at one time, take up only one thing from that list and concentrate only on that, forgetting all the other things.

As I have mentioned before, you do not have to wait for some future for your enjoyment when all your plans will be materialised. You should derive joy right now by remaining completely focussed in your present work. **Your final enjoyment of life is nothing but the sum of enjoyments of all the present moments. In other words, the real enjoyment of life doesn't depend upon the attainment of some final goal by you but it is a moment to moment enjoyment which depends on your ability to remain fully absorbed in the present activity and to perform that activity as best as you can.**

■■■

Freedom from Overtalking

If we sometimes examine our talks done during a day, we will discover that seventy five percent of these talks are non-essential, i.e., if we hadn't done that talking, no harm would have occurred.

Silence generates a lot of mental strength.

In fact, most of the talking we do is just unconscious, just out of habit, without any meaning and purpose. The impulse to talk is much stronger than many people realize. Psychologists say that the drive to talk in an unconscious state of mind in an individual is even stronger than the sex drive which is considered as the primary drive. And this impulse arises because we are restless inside and this restlessness is reflected in the form of excessive and useless talking which is a type of vomiting from our inside.

Nonessential talking does much harm to us than we often realize. For example:

1. Speaking involves expenditure of a lot of physical and mental energy which makes you tired.

2. It creates distractions in mind. A person who speaks too much is not able to focus his mind easily on any endeavour.

3. It creates friction in relationships because when you talk much, you are bound to utter some undesirable things also which may annoy and pinch another person.

4. Most of the talks you do pertain to your past and future incidents, so it throws you out of the present moment again and again and puts you with the dead experiences of the past which have already occurred or the fantasized experiences of the future which have not yet come into being.

5. Too much talking keeps you outward and prevents you from relaxing and turning inwards which is necessary for the peace of mind.

Spirituality gives a lot of importance to silence. It advises one to talk only when it is really required to communicate some useful information to the another person and this limited talking is also done in a slow, orderly, clear and sweet manner. It also emphasizes to communicate through non-verbal means as far as possible, e.g. through various facial and bodily gestures and sometimes through writing.

Silence is a great way to conserve your energy and increase the focus and concentration of your mind. It will be helpful for you to practise silence for few hours daily or even for a day sometimes. You will begin to discover through these periods of silence how extra talking is taking a toll of your useful time, energy and mental peace and creating disharmony in relationships. You will also realize that life can be very easily lived without much talking and our most of the talks are superfluous. And above all, you will start having glimpses of inner peace and joy which is the most valuable treasure of silence.

Another important benefit of silence or less talking is that there is more force in your words, when you speak. Silence increases the force and impact of your speech. That is why a man of few words creates a bigger impact on others even with his less words than a talkative person does with his lots of words.

■■■

Freedom from Unplanned, Unsystematic Working

We find around us many people who are very intelligent and can give a lot of output using their intelligence but just because of their unplanned and unsystematic working, a lot of their energy is dissipated in locating the things, in searching old data and records and then spending their time and energy to regenerate the lost things, if any.

Unplanned and unsystematic working creates a lot of stress.

I give you a very general example of an unsystematic lifestyle. Suppose, there is a phone call at your home. Some message from the caller is to be noted. But there is no notepad near the telephone. So there is a running about in the house. Somehow, you are able to come out with a piece of torn page from the copy of your child. Now there is no pen beside the telephone. So again, there is a panic among the family members to search for a pen. Finally, a pen comes but alas! it doesn't work. The second round of racing and helter-skelter begins. You can yourself imagine the scene now. You can realize that all this chaos can be simply eliminated by keeping a notepad and a pen near the telephone. So much tension, loss of energy and time for such a trifle just because of an unplanned way of living and working. Let us take up another example in the same connection. Suppose, the phone caller gives you an important message to convey it to your husband when your husband returns home at night. You say, "yes I will give". But by the time your husband comes at night, you forget to convey the message to him. When in the next day, he comes to know about this important message from somebody else, he is furious because it was an important and urgent message to be known by him yesterday itself. There is a big fight between your and your husband in the night when he returns home and your neighbours get a good entertainment, free of cost. Now all this fight could have been avoided if you had jotted down the message on the notepad near the telephone and then forgotten about it. Then it would have been your husband's duty to see this notepad when he came home, as a matter of routine.

You have also seen many examples of tension due to not finding a thing just because someone who had taken it didn't put back at the right place or a right place was not designated for a thing. There can be umpteen number of such examples where so many fights and tensions occur over such trifles which can be easily avoided just by devoting sometime in making your life planned and systematic. For example, don't let the things in your house or office be kept randomly here and there. Everything should go to its proper place instantly after use. Everything should have a designated place for its location. For keeping various loose papers and documents, generate various files. It is a very disgusting sight to see loose papers, pamphlets, letters, etc. lying on the floor, table and bed for days together.

So is the disgust I feel when I see shoes, sandals, socks, toys, towels, etc. spread all over the house instead of keeping them in proper places. In fact, it is totally based on your own common sense and intelligence as to how you organize the things. The main thing is the 'will' and 'efforts' in this direction.

By keeping things in order, you not only save your useful time and energy and avoid tension but you also feel a joy in living and working at a place where things are placed in an orderly manner.

■■■

Freedom from Negative Thoughts

People often ask me, "How to stop negative thinking?" My reply is you can't stop it by trying. The moment you leave trying there is some possibility. There are many things in life which you can't achieve by trying. Rather opposite results come by trying. Negative thinking is also one of those things. Now trying to stop negative thinking may take three forms:

I am sure I can't clear this competitive exam.

Negative thoughts tend to materialize in real life situations.

1. Fighting – you fight with them.
2. Escaping – you try to run away from them.
3. Suppression – you try to suppress the thoughts and push them from the conscious to the subconscious mind.

Now all the above measures are counter productive. Instead of weakening the negative thoughts, they will strengthen them. Why? The more the attention on a thing, the more it becomes intense. **The things you fight, the things you run away, the things you suppress, they become the centre of your attention and continuously move in your mind. This situation is something like this that the more you try to forget a thing, the more it will remain in your mind.**

Now the way to eliminate negative thinking is doing just the opposite of the above. You don't bother about the negative thinking at all. Rather focus your mind on positive thinking. Positive automatically dilutes and overcomes the negative. So the formula is that **in order to remove the negative, focus on the positive.** This situation can be better understood by an analogy. Suppose, there is a bucket filled with dirty water. If you go on pouring pure water in the bucket, eventually the bucket's water goes on being purified even without having to remove the dirty water at all.

Take another analogy. **Negative thinking is like darkness and positive thinking is like light. As soon as light falls on darkness, the darkness automatically vanishes without any direct effort on your part.** Suppose, someone goes on insisting that first I will remove darkness and then only light will be allowed to enter, you can imagine what will happen in that case. In controlled techniques of the mind, this formula of overcoming the negative is also stated as follows: **Don't focus on what you don't want. Focus on what you want.** This is because our subconscious doesn't differentiate between the two. It simply goes according to where our attention is.

Now, how to develop a positive thinking? It is a billion dollar question, easier said than done. **There is no readymade formula by which you can immediately develop a positive thinking. It is a gradual process.** The only way to develop positive thinking is to get the right knowledge and the facts of life. Unless you know the truths and realities of life properly, you can't view things in their correct perspective, i.e., as they really are. **Positive thinking is nothing but seeing things in their right perspective. Negative thinking is seeing things in a distorted manner as per your false assumptions.** To get the right knowledge of life or the reality, the whole spiritual literature is spread before you. Even all the chapters of this book are devoted to help you to develop the right understanding about life. Your own calm and conscious observation of life will also help in the attainment of this knowledge.

Another approach to eliminate negative thinking is that whenever any negative thought comes in mind, consciously observe and examine it (not trying to eliminate it but watching it) as to why it has come, from where it has come and what has prompted it? By this conscious observation, you will find that the negative thoughts have started weakening **because negative thoughts can't face conscious examination. They can flourish only when you are unconscious. So you can see that there is a difference between consciously observing the negative thoughts and remaining unconsciously immersed in negative thinking.**

I hope by now, you must have got some sort of a key for understanding and controlling the negative thoughts. However, when nothing works to get rid of a negative thought which is constantly hovering in your mind, then it is better to divert your mind to something else for sometime till you are in a position to work on that negative thought. Because a thing can trouble you only when your attention and thoughts are on that thing. But once, you have taken your attention away from that thing, then that thing (howsoever disturbing) cannot trouble you. So, diversion of mind is an effective, though temporary technique, for being away from a negative thought when nothing works.

■■■

Note: For a more scientific understanding of nature and control of thoughts, please refer my book 'How to control Mind and be Stress-free'.

Freedom from Aimless Action

Some people spend their lifetime as if they have to somehow pass the time of their life by indulging in whatever works that come on their way. **It appears as if their purpose of life is just to die one day**. They sometimes indulge in one work or project, then get bored and take up another. They

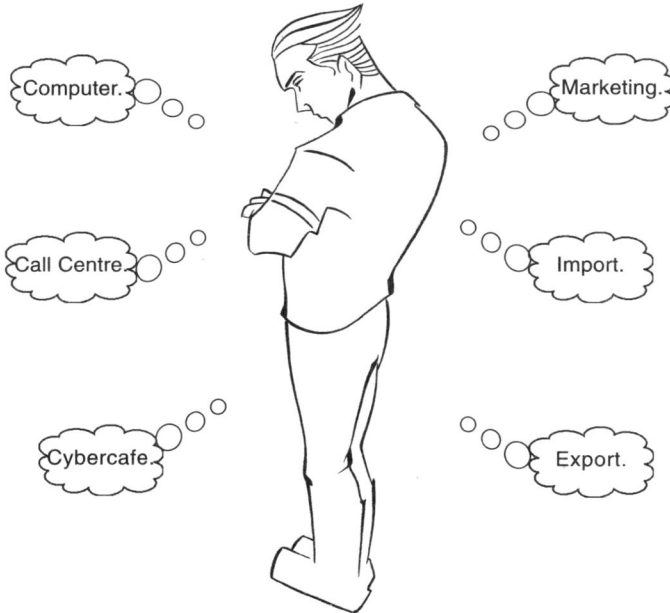

*Some persons start doing anything which comes
to their mind without any definite aim in life.*

change jobs, houses, businesses and even their friends and partners frequently. They are not clear what they want and what is their aim in life. Just whatever comes to their mind, they start doing it, get involved in it and whenever they start feeling monotonous and bored from it, they leave it as fast as they had clung to it initially. They don't have a stable centre around which to plan their activities. **Any slight attraction, distraction or jerk can move them off the Centre.**

You must understand that this life is very precious. It has not been given to us for wasting it in useless and aimless pursuits. We have not come on this earth for a vacation. **We have to achieve some purpose here. Leading life aimlessly is like kicking the football in the field here and there without aiming it towards the goal of the other party.**

You must make some short term and long term goals in your professional as well as personal life and then systematically work towards them, step by step. **All these short term and long term goals will finally become the basis to attain the highest aim of life which is 'Self-Realization'.** A directionless mind normally succumbs to its Lower Nature and becomes the victim of all types of vices and bestial instincts.

■■■

Freedom from the Attitude of Resistance

If you observe the tendencies of the people towards the happenings of life, you will find that most of us are simply resisting what is happening to us. And this resistance is expressed in the form of complaints, criticisms, blames, irritation, hatred, frustration and so many other ways. **Very few people exist on this earth who accept everything**

Attitude of non-acceptance is the biggest source of stress in our life.

whether good or bad, pleasant or unpleasant, adverse or favourable with a calm and stable mind. One of the key formula for being peaceful and at ease in life is, first of all, to accept everything. Only after acceptance, you can

139

take the next step as to what you can do to alleviate this suffering or unpleasantness. But unless you take the first step of acceptance, how will you take the second step properly?

The principle of acceptance is based on the fact that anything can happen in life. **Life is open ended from all sides and all possibilities exist for anything to happen. You should be ready for any eventuality no matter how tragic, catastrophic, awful or terrible it may be**. You may get a serious or incurable disease; you may become old; your wife and children may leave you; you can die one day; you may have accidents; your friends and relatives may leave and cheat you, etc. All these things are possible and you should be able to accept them.

But what are people doing? They say with astonishment and wonder, "Oh! I had never thought in my young age that I will become old one day, that I will die one day, that my children will leave me and I will be left alone in my old age, that I will develop this disease, that my relatives will cheat me, that I will be so unlucky in business" and so on. Not only this, people are also showing resistance in the form of complaining, criticizing and blaming bureaucrats, politicians, government departments, etc. for corruption, cheating, dishonesty, inefficiency, carelessness and so on. You can realize that by singing this song, nothing happens except that you are charged with negative feelings inside you because this is not the way for changing a bad person or a bad system.

Resistance always creates tension, unease, hatred and frustration. On the other hand, acceptance (and the belief that anything can happen in life) creates a feeling of relief, peace and ease as if a heavy load has been lifted off from your shoulders. **Acceptance of everything with all humility and gratefulness towards God is one of the greatest keys for ascending the spiritual ladder.**

■■■

Freedom from Panic

There are many people who are expert in creating a panic whenever any challenge, adversity, problem and slightest misfortune hits them. It is a kind of habit or mindset for them to act in this manner rather than the real seriousness of the situation. In our life, many sad events may take place

Oh! What will happen if the train is missed?

By saying such statements, this person is creating panic among others also.

but they can't create a panic inside us unless we make a catastrophe out of them by thinking that this is the end of the world or this is the most important thing of life or a life and death situation has arrived.

But is it so? Is anything in life really so terrible? **Experience of thousands of enlightened men who themselves faced many storms of life shows that there is nothing in this life which can be called catastrophic or unbearable. Everything can be accepted and handled with serenity.** Showing reasonable concern over a sad event and taking remedial measures is quite alright. It is the overconcern and overanxiety which creates panic.

It is only when we start taking things unduly serious and giving them more weightage than what they deserve that they start dominating us. Give only that much importance to a thing which it deserves. If you can learn to view the things from a distance with a larger perspective, you will find that things are not as terrible as you imagined them from a narrow perspective. So next time, when you get disturbed in life by something, just ask yourself, "If this thing is really that important or serious so as to make you so much disturbed? If this is the most important thing in your life? What is the value of this thing compared to the overall goal of your life?" You will find that this very questioning and challenging will unload your mind from the unwanted disturbance.

We give below an example to show how to decatastrophize any situation to reduce your panic. For example, suppose, you are feeling panicky about an interview, you have to appear tomorrow. Just ask yourself, what it is that you are feeling so nervous about? Is it because you are afraid that you won't be able to reply all the questions? How does it matter if you are not able to reply the interviewer's questions? At the most, you won't be selected. So what? Heavens will not fall. You will not become a beggar on the street. If you are afraid that the interviewers will consider you a fool, then what will happen even if they think so? There are many fools in the world including greater fools than you. Is it going to make any difference to the world even if you are a fool? Will the world become standstill because of this fact? Then why are you so perturbed?

So, this way by questioning and challenging your anxieties, you can decatastrophize any situation and reduce your panic. As mentioned earlier, **taking things seriously and emotionally also builds strong impressions in our subconscious mind**. These impressions then make us more susceptible to surrender in the face of similar situations in future. Hence, try to face every situation in life maintaining a complete control, stability and consciousness of the mind and don't allow yourself to react unconsciously.

■ ■ ■

Freedom from False Prayers

I know that you may be shocked to read this title because all the religions continuously exhort you to pray to God.

But I have used the term 'prayer' in a different sense in which most of the people use it. Most of the people use the term 'prayer' in the form of begging from God. Somebody is demanding a job for his/her son. Somebody is

Oh God! please make my business flourish. I will distribute a prasad of Rs 1000/- if you fulfil my wish.

We are ready to give bribe to God also if He fulfils our wish.
In the name of prayer, we make a mockery of God.

demanding a good match for his daughter's marriage. Somebody wants good results in examination, etc. We call all this as prayer in today's world.

And on the top of this, we also assure God to give some bribe if our desire is fulfilled in the form of some donation, some food or some *prasad* to a temple. This is the height of making a mockery of our prayers.

I am talking of freedom from such type of prayers which are nothing but asking from God like a beggar as if God doesn't know what your needs are and what you need to be given. Please remember that **you get from God what you deserve and not what you ask for.**

Real prayer is not demanding from God but thanking God for what He has given us. **Real prayer is just thankfulness and total acceptance of what has been provided to you by God.** What you have been provided by God is much more than what you deserve and what you desire.

■■■

Freedom from Duality of the World

The definition of the word, 'world' is that which is dual in nature. Creation is built on the principle of duality, meaning thereby that everything here is made of two opposite aspects; such as day-night, life-death, summer-winter, male-female, young-old, pleasure-pain, joy-sorrow, association-disassociation, etc.

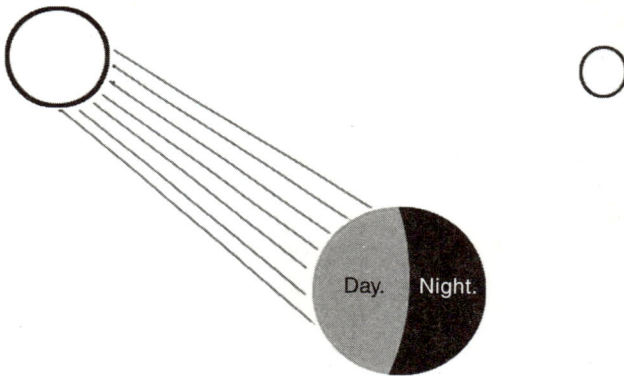

Creation is built of two opposite aspects which keep it in dynamic balance.

These two aspects can't be separated from each other. They are inbuilt in the nature of worldly things. They are the two faces of the same coin. In fact, these two aspects are complementary to each other rather than antagonistic, i.e., one aspect can't work alone without the existence of the another aspect. Can you imagine day without night, male without female, young without old or life without death. You can imagine the chaos if only one part is allowed to function in nature. In fact, **nature maintains a dynamic balance with the simultaneous existence of these two**

opposite aspects, what is called *Yin* and *Yang* in Chinese terminology. Now if you want that there should be only the day (not night), only the light (not darkness), only the life (not death), only the youth (not old age), then you are bound to suffer.

Not only in the case of nature, there is duality in this respect also that if you are having some advantages, comforts and pleasures from something, some place or some person in this world, you will also have corresponding disadvantages, discomforts and problems from them of some kind. For example, when you marry, you have certain pleasures and advantages but you have certain disadvantages too in the form of additional responsibilities, adjustments, etc. You buy a house somewhere. You have certain advantages but also certain anxieties and tensions associated with its upkeep, maintenance, legal aspects, etc. Any person or thing which associates with you must also dissociate or leave you at sometime. If you have got some gain or profit sometime, you may also suffer loss at some other time. So this happens with everything. Sometimes, people see only one aspect of a thing and make a hasty conclusion that it is very good or bad. But actually, they forget to see the opposite aspect. This is why, it is said that **what appears is not always the reality**.

The reason of our suffering is that we cling to pleasures and become repulsive to pain. In everything, we want to hold on to the pleasurable and comfortable aspects and push the painful and the uncomfortable aspects away, i.e., we want that only pleasure should remain with us and not the pain. In other words, we just want to separate out the pleasure from pain in everything which is practically impossible because it will violate the law of the divine balance in the world. According to this law if you want to avoid pains and discomforts in your life, you will have to leave the desire for pleasures and comforts also. If you don't want insult, you will have to leave the desire for praise also.

147

The best way to remain unaffected by this dual nature of the world is to deal with worldly things and incidents with a detached outlook as if you are merely a spectator, i.e., neither get elated in success nor grieved in failure. Remain evenminded in gain/loss, success/failure, praise/ insult, etc. *Yoga* recommends dispassion and non-attachment towards both pleasure and pain, i.e., neither undue craving for pleasure nor aversion for pain. *Yoga* encourages healthy enjoyment of pleasures and using material objects for our comforts but to avoid becoming unduly attached to them. Similarly, *Yoga* encourages facing pains and discomforts with equanimity and balance of mind with no attempt to resist and escape. Once you reach to this mental level, you become free from the clutches of dualities.

The principle of duality also gives us a valuable lesson to follow in our practical life that we should not be overfussy or overchoosy while taking a decision in any worldly matter because no matter what we choose, everything will have some pros ad cons. So just make a decision (whether it be a job, selection of a bride or an article to be purchased from market) based on normal search and inspection and then try to find satisfaction and contentment in whatever you have.

Everlasting happiness or bliss which is free from any duality or the opposite aspects comes from inside, the deep recesses of your inner Self (the divine spark or the spirit inside you). This is what we should strive to get through meditation and other practices of *Yoga* for our everlasting happiness.

■■■

Freedom from Haphazard and Random Thinking

The minds of most of the people runs with a tremendous velocity with one thought followed by other like one car bumping into another in a high traffic area. Their minds are not still even for a moment. Their thoughts are moving randomly from here to there without any direction.

Random thoughts moving in mind drain a lot of your energy.

Haphazard thinking is an unconscious phenomena. If you are unconscious, your mind moves haphazardly by its very nature. The way to remove this tendency is to become again and again conscious of your thoughts and assert that you

149

will do only planned thinking. You are not suggesting your mind to stop thoughts but to think in a planned and orderly manner instead of thinking haphazardly. **As you learn to be more and more conscious of your thoughts, you will find that your mind has slowed down**. Slowing down your mind essentially means reducing the number of thoughts in your mind per unit of time. Suppose, previously one thousand thoughts used to move across your mind in a minute and now only hundred thoughts move in the same time, it means you have slowed down your mind to that extent. **The number of thoughts moving across your mind per unit of time indicates the velocity of the mind. When your mind is moving haphazardly, the number of thoughts moving across your mind per unit of time is very high**.

The high velocity of the mind or the tremendous rush of thoughts in your mind is a sign of weak and uncontrolled mind. A controlled mind can continue to keep only one thought for as long as it desires without allowing other thoughts to come in. It may even remain thoughtless for a period of time, it desires.

Now the practical way to reduce the velocity of the mind is to consciously bring it again and again in the present moment and not allow it to be unconsciously sucked in the past and the future. You will notice that as the velocity of the mind decreases and so the number of thoughts, the amount of peace, joy and bliss increases proportionately in the mind.

Further, another thing which is to be noted is that **the lesser the thoughts in your mind, the more is the power of your thought which you think. So there is an inverse relationship between the quantity and quality of thinking**. If you learn to remain thoughtless for sometime daily, the power of your thoughts will increase tremendously.

■■■

Freedom from Insecurity and Fear

If you observe around yourself, you will find that the maximum portion of time of the people is aimed at removing insecurities from their life. You somehow want to come to that state where you are totally safe and secure in life. You build properties, make huge bank balance, invest in long term savings, take so many insurance policies, create family, create friends, build relationships, etc., all to ensure that your future will be totally safe and secure.

Insecurity about the future is the major source of fear.

151

But one earthquake, one tsunami, one cyclone or one war and all your dreams for safety are shattered to pieces. Just one minute of the fury of nature can reduce everything to ashes. We are too small before this vast existence.

The truth of life is that life is full of so many uncertainties that you can't create a foolproof security here for yourself. **No matter what you do, life continues to remain insecure by its very nature. The only way to go beyond the fears of insecurity is, first of all, to accept the fact of the insecurity of life and not fight with this reality. The second thing is to know that permanent security can come only from God and not from any material means.** If you always remain linked to God, always feel His association with you, always feel His hand and control everywhere in the world, you will gradually start feeling secure in this insecure world.

This is not to say that one must not take any measures for his future. What we mean to say is that one must not be obsessive about his security. One must accept that there are dangers in life and you can't eliminate all the dangers from your life. You can overcome these dangers only by joining hands with God because God is definitely above all dangers and He can control anything and everything.

Another point to be kept in mind is that fears or anxieties of various insecurities and dangers crop up in or your mind when you habitually transport yourself in to the future. Fears don't exist in the present moment. They are the product of your thinking about the future. **So if you learn to remain in the present moment for the maximum time, most of the fears about your future insecurities will automatically vanish.** This is not to say that you shouldn't do any future planning for yourself. You must do that but after doing a reasonable planning.

Spoiling your present for making your future better can be the greatest foolishness of your life.

Freedom from Competition and Race

One of the ways we keep our children and young generation stressed is to infuse in them a great feeling of competition which keeps them involved in a rat race with others. Now what is competition? The meaning of competition is that you have to go ahead in comparison with others. As soon as the word 'comparison' comes, we have introduced the element of stress inside them.

You have to come first in the class, come what may.

Competition generates feelings of jealousy, selfishness and anxiety among children.

A person who is in comparison with others can't remain without stress because he is always anxious and on his toes that somebody may leave him behind. And out of so many persons, only one person can be at the top and not all. So one who is in competition will do all sorts of manipulations, cheating and foul play so that others may not come up to his stage. It is surprising to see parents pumping their children that they have to come first in the class. Now every child's parents are saying this and only one child will come first out of all of them. So you can imagine the state of mind of the remaining children and parents after the result.

There can be another way whereby our children can be better educated without getting stressed. You can encourage the child to read more from the consideration of gaining knowledge and not from the consideration of competing with anyone. You should tell your children that ranking and positions in class are unimportant and the main thing is the understanding and knowledge of the subject. Then all that pressure of competition will go away and the interest in gaining knowledge will increase. And once, they get good knowledge, then good marks will automatically follow as a byproduct without any direct anxiety or tension for the same.

■■■

Freedom from Ego Based Pleasures

The term 'ego' when used in general sense refers to our **Lower nature.** Ego based pleasures are pleasures of our Lower nature and therefore, they are harmful to us and should be avoided.

Ego based pleasures are those pleasures which provide stimulation and excitement to our body and mind.

Instead of ego based pleasures, we should strive to get joy of our inner Self though various spiritual practices.

They are also called *Rajasik* pleasures. Examples of such pleasures are:

  i) Craving for name, fame, recognition, power, status (i.e. feeling of superiority), etc.

 ii) Always searching for some company (can't remain alone).

iii) Tendency to talk continuously and do conversations (can't remain silent).

 iv) Eating stimulating foods and drinks.

v) Watching sensational movies (containing horror, violence, suspense, sex, etc.).

vi) Hearing stimulating songs and music (e.g. Pop, Disco, Rock music, etc.).

vii) Reading & hearing sensational news from newspapers and T.V. relating to violence, accidents, rape, political reshuffle, various scams and scandals, natural calamities, terrorist attacks, dacoities, bomb blasts, etc.

viii) Watching adventurous and risky undertakings and sports by people, e.g. risky driving, adventurous climbing, risky swimming, etc.

ix) Making comments, criticisms, ridicule, sarcastic remarks on others and their works.

x) Participating in political discussions, negative comments on politicians judging their performances, bonafides and integrity and relishing the same.

xi) Taking interest to find out about the private and confidential things of other persons in office/ neighbourhood and discussing them with one another.

xii) Spreading rumours and exaggerating and distorting the facts to make them more spicy and exciting.

xiii) Leaking statements, remarks and comments of one person about the another person.

On the surface, all the above look great pleasures to our ego but these pleasures also have an opposite side in the form of pain because of inherent duality of these pleasures. This pain may come because of many factors involved in these types of pleasures, e.g.

(a) Firstly, for enjoying these pleasures, you have to depend on others and depending on others always causes misery because the 'other' may change or vanish anytime.

(b) Secondly, these pleasures are addictive in nature. You are not satisfied with whatever amount you get. The more you get, the more you want.

(c) These ego or Lower nature based pleasures give you only excitement and stimulations, keeping you in a state of restlessness and agitation. They don't provide rest and peace to the mind. Living continuously in a state of stimulation harms both the body and mind because our body and mind need some rest also. Sometimes, as a reaction of overexcitement, people go to the other extreme and take such drugs and eatables which make them drowsy and forgetful about themselves.

Spirituality encourages the joy of *Higher nature* which comes from our inner Self. While excitement belongs to an extreme, joy and bliss of the inner Self belongs to the middle, i.e., in this joy, you feel restful, stable and not hyper. As I have explained in chapter 48, the ego's emotions always remain in extremes (from hyper to hopo and from hypo to hyper) while positive emotions originating from our real Self belong to the middle.

Through various spiritual practices, such as Yoga and meditation, we should awaken our inner Self for this inner joy to come forth. Once this inner joy emerges, you will no longer need any outward excitements to lead your life. They will fall off by themselves in the face of emergence of the Higher nature. You can also have a glimpse of this inner joy by consciously practising various divine virtues in your day-to-day life because divine virtues trigger the real Self (Divine virtues are the attributes of the real Self only).

■■■

Freedom from *Siddhis* and Occult Powers

In *Yoga*, we frequently hear of many *siddhis* and psychic powers acquired by the *yogis* after a period of intense *sadhana* and practice of austerity. Some of them are listed below:

1. Clairvoyance (remote viewing).

2. Clairaudience (remote hearing).

3. Telepathy (transmission of thoughts at great distances from one mind to another).

4. Telekinesis (movement of objects solely through mind power).

5. Levitation – (lifting of body in the air).

6. Dematerialization of body and rematerialization at a distant location.

7. Apport phenomena (Transporting material objects through space by the process of dematerialization and rematerialization).

8. Increasing or decreasing the size and weight of body.

9. Out of body travel.

10. Disappearance and emergence of objects from nowhere.

A layman confuses all these powers with spirituality and considers a person highly spiritual if he can display these powers more and more.

Please note that all these powers belong to the mind (subconscious mind) and not to the 'Self' (which is the spiritual element inside us also called the soul or spirit). A spiritual person can definitely show these powers but he will have to come down to the level of his mind. A really enlightened person will never show his powers to others for pleasing and impressing people and to prove his high status. Such type of desires belongs to the ego and not to the Self.

A spiritual person shows any of the above mentioned powers only when it is demanded by the situation for the welfare of all. Further, if a person starts

Psychic powers of a yogi reduce when he starts displaying them in public like a magician.

showing these powers in an egoistic manner, gradually, his powers decrease and he declines to a lower level. We have seen many instances where a spiritual person has fallen to low levels just because of misuse of these powers.

So you should be very clear in mind that spirituality and occultism/psychicism are two different things and a person showing occult powers needn't be a person of high moral character. You should also shun such display of powers if you seem to develop any during your spiritual journey because these powers are just byproducts of your journey towards the spiritual growth and are not the goal of spirituality.

■■■

Freedom from Junk Foods

Junk foods are those foods which have lost their naturalness. They are made by refining, processing and mixing of colours, chemicals and preservatives in the original food materials obtained from nature.

Our body is a part of nature and has been made in such a fashion that it can very well accept and assimilate natural foods fully without any harmful side effects. But as soon as you make some alterations in the nature's original substances, some side effects and harms are bound to occur in our system.

Consumption of junk food is incresing day by day in youngsters.

For example, take the case of white sugar or table sugar. It is manufactured by refining and processing of sugarcanes. In the process of refining, it is deprived of all its vitamins, minerals and fibres and becomes empty of calories. Now for the metabolism of sugar, the body needs these vitamins and minerals. So the body now takes these nutrients from the various places in the body itself, e.g., bones, nerves, muscles, skin, eyes, etc. and the result is vitamin and mineral (especially calcium) deficiency in the body leading to various problems like weak bones, nervous irritability, tiredness, muscular diseases, poor eye sight, etc.

Further, pure sugar immediately increases the blood glucose level, which is followed by sugar low after sometime as a reaction of insulin produced in the body and this creates a feeling of fatigue, depression and body aches. Natural foods are never designed to produce this sudden high and sudden low in the body. Similarly, absence of fibres in refined sugar creates other types of problems like constipation, fast absorption of sugar in the intestines, increase in cholesterol uptake by the intestine, etc. Further, the addition of harmful chemicals for producing colour, flavour and for the preservation of foods create various toxins and poisons in the body and the body has to work hard to eliminate these toxins. New researches prove that these chemicals are cancerous too. Like sugar, we can explain the bad effects of all the junk foods. Most common constituents of junk foods are :

1. White sugar
2. White Salt
3. White flour (*maida*)
4. Caeffeine
5. Artificial chemicals (for colour, flavour and preservatives)
6. Excess fat in fried form (dalda, butter, vegetable oil, etc.)

However, the main things to keep in mind is that as soon as you deviate from the natural organic foods, the body is going to react with some harmful repercussions.

For the benefit of readers, I am listing some of the junk foods below so that you may attempt to reduce their consumption as much as possible:

1. Pizza
2. Burger
3. White bread
4. Biscuit, cookies

5. Pastries, cakes, cream rolls
6. Patties
7. Nans
8. Noodles
9. Chocolates, toffees, candy
10. Tea, coffee
11. Various fried *namkeens*
12. Squashes, *sharbats*
13. Chips, friams, *papad*
14. Sweets
15. Jams, jelly
16. Tinned/Canned vegetables, fruits and fruit juices
17. Sauce, Ketchups
18. Pickles
19. *Pakoras, Samosas*
20. Soft drinks, etc.

It is not necessary to avoid these food items completely. You can take them occasionally because the body has the capacity to tolerate them in small quantity without any ill effects. Only thing is that their regular and excessive consumption should be avoided. Here are some natural foods for which you should develop your taste as your primary foods.

1. Fruits
2. Vegetables
3. Nuts (Almonds, peanuts, cashewnuts, walnuts, *pista*)
4. Sprouted pulses
5. Whole grain cereals and pulses and many more such natural foods.

■■■

Note: For more elaborate and scientific details of junk foods, please refer my book *Foods that are killing you*.

Freedom from Overmedication

Our age is characterized by an indiscriminate use of medicines. The medical sector attracts the maximum amount of money from consumers. Billions of dollars are spent in the production and consumption of medicines every year.

Excessive medication does more harm than good.

The excessive use of medicines causes more harm to the body than benefits. The reason being that for the body, the medicine (allopathic) is a foreign agent. The body accepts only natural organic materials for incorporation in the body while allopathic medicines are mostly inorganic. Hence the body starts removing the medicine from the system as soon as you take it. That's why kidneys and liver which play a

163

vital role in elimination of foreign substances from the blood are overtaxed and are worst affected by excess medications. This is the reason why we have to take the daily dose of medicine because the earlier dose of medicine is eliminated from the body after sometime.

Secondly, any medicine you take, it moves in the blood throughout the body in addition to the place where it is required to work. Hence, it causes unnecessary side effects at other places in addition to its effect on the primary site. Thirdly, these medications are only symptomatic, i.e., **they only remove the undesirable symptoms of the disease and not the disease itself. In other words, they work only on the 'effects' and not on the 'cause'.** Since the root cause of the disease is not eliminated or rather suppressed, the disease reoccurs again and again in different forms and rather converts into a chronic ailment.

However, we cannot say that medical science is of no use to us. In fact, in emergency, the allopathic medicines and other tools of modern medical science are a boon since they work very fast on the symptoms of a disease compared to any other system of therapy. What we mean to say is that their consumption on regular basis for normal and chronic ailments should be reduced because they don't work on the root causes.

For chronic ailments, one should resort to nature cure treatments (e.g. Yoga, Exercises, Diet therapy, Fasting, Pranayam, Accupressure, Hydrotherapy, Colour therapy, Swara Yoga, Sound therapy, Mudras, etc.) These alternative therapies go from 'effect' to the 'cause' and make changes at the causal level which result in permanent cure. Further in the nature cure, there are no harmful side effects on the body. This is also called **holistic treatment** since by nature cure, not only the primary problem is treated but the whole body gets a face lift because according to the universal principles **"Every part is connected to the 'whole' and the 'whole' is connected to every 'part'. No part of the**

body is an island in itself". So when you do anything to any part of the body, the effect is transmitted to the whole body. Similarly, when you do something to the whole body, the effect goes to other parts too.

I remember a beautiful anecdote. On being asked to a nature cure specialist by someone that "If people leave using medicines, how the persons connected to the medical profession will survive?" The nature cure specialist replied, "You continue to buy medicines, so that they (medical personnel) are saved but throw all these medicines in the sea so that you are saved".

■■■

Note: For yoga and nature cure treatments of various chronic diseases, you can refer my following books:

  (i)   A layman's Guide to Chronic Diseases

  (ii) A layman's Guide for Heart Care

  (iii) Freedom from cervical and Back Pain – the natural way

  (iv) Healing through Reiki – an experience with life energy

Freedom from Artificial Lifestyle

Our 21st century lifestyle is characterized by a highly modern lifestyle full of comforts and luxuries. Although we may claim that we have all types of facilities to lead a comfortable life, but if we look deeply, we will find that this lifestyle is highly artificial and not close to nature.

Artificial life style upsets the balance of body giving birth to many life style diseases.

It is a fundamental law that as soon as we deviate from nature in any comfort or luxury, some harmful consequences, repercussions or side effects are bound to arise. Artificial or man-made things can never equate with nature. Let us illustrate with some examples the difference between natural and artificial living.

1.   In winter, you want heat for your comfort. In one option, you can get this heat by sitting in winter sun and in another option, you can get this heat by

a room heater or convector, sitting inside a closed room. Although scientifically, both are heat but in terms of the effect on your body, there is enormous difference between the two. Room heater or convector (an artificial thing) has harmful effects on your body while the sun's heat has beneficial effects on your health. You can yourself feel the difference between the two.

2. In summer, using desert cooler is more natural than air conditioner which has harmful effects by recycling the same air again and again.

3. Drinking chilled water from the fridge is an artificial way of quenching thirst and has harmful effect on the body while drinking natural water from a river, mountain and stored in a pitcher (for coolness) is natural and beneficial.

4. Eating raw or steamed/boiled vegetables is more natural than cooked and fried ones using a lot of fat in the form of cooking oil and butter.

5. Walking/strolling in the garden and sitting under a tree for fresh air is more natural and beneficial than sitting in a closed room and inhaling conditioned air from an air conditioner.

6. Eating vegetarian food is more natural than non-vegetarian and processed food.

7. Remaining in open space with more sunlight and ventilation is more natural than living in a closed room without windows and having only artificial lights.

8. Listening to soft music (e.g. old melodious songs; classical music, *bhajans*/ devotional songs) is more natural than modern pop, rock and disco music.

9. Eating and talking while seeing T.V., eating while lying on bed, continuously eating some snacks or

the other, eating late dinner, etc. comes under artificial life. In natural living, you eat at the right time and at regular intervals and don't eat while talking, reading and watching television.

10. Reading stimulating and spicy literature/articles/stories, reading while lying down, all come under artificial living. In natural living, you read in a proper posture sitting on a chair only and you like to read thought-provoking and creative articles, which give nourishment to your soul.

11. Immediately, after waking up in the morning, taking bed tea, reading newspaper, opening the television for news, sports, movies, etc. all come under artificial living and are harmful for your psyche and *soma*. One should eat anything in the morning only after attending natural calls and cleaning the mouth and should keep his mind relatively silent and free from any distractions at that time.

12. Drinking fruit juices, lemon honey, sugarcane juice, *lassi*, milkshakes, *thandai*, etc. are more natural beverages than cola drinks and various artificial *sharbats* and squashes. And of course, alcohol is a big 'no'.

13. Sleeping and waking up at irregular times, waking up in the night, sleeping in daytime, etc. also come under artificial living.

It is also to be noted that in natural living, you draw a lot of vital energy or *prana* from natural substances since nature is filled with *prana* which increases the vitality of your body. The functioning of your body depends upon the vital energy in your body. Artificial things are devoid of *prana* or life energy.

■■■

Freedom from Pessimism, Hopelessness and Depression

It is observed that many people develop the attitude of pessimism, hopelessness and become depressed when some big loss, tragedy or misfortune strikes them in life. They feel they are helpless and a victim and are just doomed. They think that they have no power to do anything and improve their lot. This feeling comes from the ignorance of the basic laws of the universe which are stated below:

Persismism and feeling of hopelessness is a negative frame of mind.

1. **Each of our lives will have dark days. And each dark day will pass by. It has always been and will always be so.** Nothing worldly lasts forever. Most troubles unless recalled in mind again and again last but for a little while. You can face any hardship by saying to yourself that **This, too, shall pass away**.

So when confronted with the darkness and the inevitable, accept it as a part of life. Let our dark days pass by but don't renew the darkness again and again in your mind on successive tomorrows. **"Let the dead past bury its dead".**

There is much inner strength in knowing that the darkest day will surely pass. There is a famous quote, **"When it gets darkest, the stars come out".** Stories of the lives of many great men are the living examples of this truth.

I would like to quote an example from the life of Abraham Lincoln in this regard. Dale Carnegie, who spent three years doing research on Lincoln's life and writing his biography wrote that Lincoln became dangerously ill in body and mind and sank into deep and terrible spell of melancholy, mumbling incoherent sentences and threatening suicide. He even wrote a poem about suicide and had it published in one of the *Springfield* papers. His friends took his knife away from him to keep him from killing himself.

Yet when it was the darkest period for Abraham Lincoln, in some mysterious way, the stars came out. You can see those stars now in the greatness of Lincoln's presidential years and how much his life bestowed upon the nation. Lincoln changed the destiny of America by lighting the way of Americans towards freedom, equality, justice and brotherhood for all. In **Springfield Illinois**, Lincoln's old home is preserved as a national shrine.

2. Another law of life is that when one door closes, another opens. **All the doors are never closed for anyone no matter how wicked and bad a person may have been. No one is doomed to eternal hell.** Everyone is given a chance to improve and come out of the vicious cycle of the law of *karma*.

But we spend too much time looking with regret at the closed door instead of searching for the open door. When life gently closes its door on a dark day, you should seek and find a newly opened door, through which you can walk courageously into a brighter tomorrow. **The door to the future always awaits you.**

3. **One amazing law of life is that you are never given a burden more than you are able to bear.** It is only when you cling to an old burden and carry the weight of yesterdays along with the burden of each new day, that you falter and break. Sufficient are the burdens of each day and sufficient is your strength for each day's burden. You should affirm, **"I stood yesterday; I can stand today; I will stand tomorrow"**.

Contemplating on these basic laws of life will help you to come out of your self-made enclosure of despair, hopelessness and pessimism.

■■■

Freedom from Wrong Postures and Gestures

Many people don't realize how our various body postures and gestures may have an effect on our moods or mental states. For manifestation of any mental state, you have to adopt a particular posture and gesture otherwise that mental state is not possible. It has been rightly said, "**As the posture, so the mood**". For example, try to be angry while in the 'namaskar' pose (posture in which you fold hands in front of your chest while greeting somebody). It will be impossible for you to remain angry in this *mudra*. For anger to continue, the body has to maintain a certain posture and gesture, otherwise the anger can't persist.

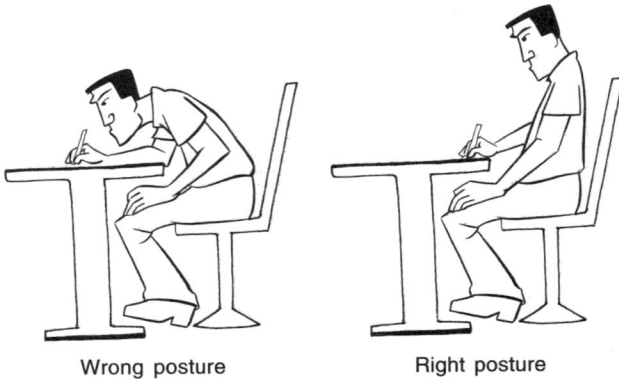

Wrong posture   Right posture

Take another example. Try to sit, stand and walk with your spine, neck and head straight and body centered and symmetrical. Now do the same with the spine and neck bent (i.e., not in a straight line) and the body unsymmetrical about its centre (i.e., bent in a particular way). Feel the difference in your self confidence and energy in both the cases. You will find that in the first case, when the spine is erect and the body is centered, your mental state is of alertness and confidence while in the other case, it is of drowsiness and shakiness. Let us have one more example. Put a smiling gesture on your face. Now try to think of some negative thoughts or have negative feelings. You will find it impossible.

The lesson from the above examples is that in your daily life, you can consciously try to maintain these postures and gestures which help you to keep a positive mental state. This will help you in ways more than one as mentioned below:

(i) This will boost or accelerate your efforts to develop a positive outlook in all the life's situations.

(ii) This will prevent or at least delay the development of negative mental states in adverse situations. In other words, your tendency of being disturbed in various negative circumstances will decrease.

(iii) Last but not the least, right postures will do immensely to boost your physical health. For example, you must be knowing the significance of maintaining a straight spine while sitting, standing and lying which helps tremendously in proper functioning of the internal body organs and in keeping your backbone healthy, thus keeping you youthful and energetic for long.

I may also mention here that 'Yoga' also speaks of various finger *mudras* in which by joining various fingers with each other, we manipulate the five elements (earth, water, air, fire and the sky or *akasa*) within our body and remove the imbalances of these elements. Imbalance of these elements in our body creates specific body problems and specific mental tendencies which are set right by practising the relevant *mudras* specific to these imbalances.

Since details of various postures and *mudras* is not possible in this book, the readers who may be interested in going in further detail, may refer my following books:

1. *Freedom from cervical and back pain* — Chapter no. 3 titled, ***Good postures to avoid backache and cervical pain.***

2. *Healing through Reiki* — Chapter no. 13 titled, ***Balancing panch pranas.***

■■■

Freedom from Harshness in Speech

There are many people whose voice and speech are very harsh and rough and one feels unpleasant and uncomfortable while talking to such persons. The tone of their voice is such as if somebody is constantly hitting your head with stones. On the other hand, there are some people whose voice is so sweet that you feel like constantly listening to them. Their words provide a soothing effect on the listener as if he is having a pleasant bath in the soothing waters of a river.

Of course, the reason of talking in a rough language and tone is mostly the inner state of mind (Apart from the effect of the surroundings and the environment in which one has grown up). When a person develops the attitude of hostility and dislike against everyone and views everything negatively, he is always in a reactive and aggressive mood which is expressed in his tone also. Further, when a person's mind is not stable and wavering here and there in a confused manner, doing things in a hurry and in a, rush his voice also can't be pleasing.

Sweet voice is invariably associated with good and loving gesture.

175

Apart from trying to change one's mental state and attitude from negative to positive, one can take the following measures for making his or her voice sweet and amiable.

1. **Silence**: The less you speak and the more you remain silent, the sweetness and force of your speech increases. So develop the habit of speaking less and to the point.

2. **OM and GUNJAN Pranayama**: Take a deep breath and then utter 'Om' through your mouth while exhaling as long as possible. Do this ten times. In *Gunjan Pranayama*, take a deep breath and while exhaling, utter the humming sounds (like that of bees) from your throat with lips closed for as long as possible. Do this ten times.

3. **Vowel Sounds**: Like the above *pranayama*, take a deep breath and utter the elongated vowel sound (e.g. a, o, oo, aa, e, etc.) with long exhalation.

4. **Chanting**: Chant various *mantras* with clapping and musical instruments, if possible. Vibrations of the *mantras* are very helpful for making your mind positive as well as making your voice sweet. Some popular *mantras* for chanting are :

(i) Gayatri mantra

(ii) *Sri Ram jai Ram, jai jai Ram*

(iii) *Hare Ram hare Ram, Ram Ram hare hare or*

    Hare Krishna hare Krishna, Krishna Krishna hare hare

(iv) *Om namo bhagvate Vasudevaya*

(v) *Om namo Shivaya*

(vi) *Hari om namo Narayana*

5. **Singing**: Singing songs where you have to stretch your voice with long exhalation helps a lot in making your voice sweet and melodious.

6. **Speak slowly**: Deliberately develop the habit of speaking at a slow pace with focus on each word and sentence and the gaps in between. The habit of speaking fast destroys the grace and beauty of the speech.

7. **Positive Gestures**: Gestures have a great link with a sweet voice. If you maintain a smiling, loving and relaxed gesture on your face, your words are bound to be sweet and will leave a soothing influence on others.

■■■

Freedom from Pride and Arrogance

Pride and arrogance are also termed as Ego or *Ahamkara* in technical parlance. In a layman's language, this feeling implies that "I am somebody. I am not an ordinary person". Ego is said to be the greatest stumbling block in the spiritual growth of a person. Swami Sivananda says, **"Ego is the wall between you and God. As soon as the ego dissolves, you come face to face with God."**

Pride and arrogance make the person blind towards others, problems and needs.

An arrogant and proudy person is not able to see the larger pattern and scheme of life. He fails to understand that the universe and our life, both are controlled and sustained by a much higher power and we are just a speck of dust in this infinitely vast existence. **We are a momentary wave in the eternity of time and space.** We can also observe it practically when the nature shows its fury in the form of floods, cyclone, earthquakes, tsunami, etc. and we feel like helpless victims at that time.

Before that larger power (God), we are so tiny that it looks ridiculous to have even the slightest pride and arrogance in our separate personal power. Spirituality advises us that instead of showing your separate power, you should surrender to that Higher Power and flow with Him, flow with life, flow with nature, rather than flowing against them. No matter how much you try, the 'part' can never win against the 'whole'. In this fight against the whole, the 'part' can only be destroyed'. A 'part' can only enjoy when it works hand in hand with the 'whole'. Then it can also share the power of the 'whole'.

That is why, all spiritually realized persons pray this to God. "Not mine, only Thy will be done". In fact, at this stage, all personal power, personal goals and personal desires are left behind. A spiritual person works for the 'whole', for all of us rather than for 'me and mine' as a co-partner and servant of God.

In fact, when your ego dissolves, God is then able to get a chance to work through you because ego is the only barrier between you and God. It is the experience of all mystics that when ego dissolves, it appears to them that they are not doing anything. It is God who is working through them and things are simply happening through them. They are only being used as a channel, an instrument or a *'nimmit'*. They are simply allowing life to flow through them effortlessly like a river without any resistance. The feeling that they are somebody totally vanishes. Rather, they feel that when alone, they are nobody or zero and only in association with God, they are something.

Pride and arrogance lead to the definite downfall of a person, sooner or later. Our entire history is filled with such examples.

■■■

Freedom from Nervousness

Nervousness is generated out of the feeling of self-inadequacy and generally, indicates a lack of self-confidence in you. You don't have trust and faith in your capability and power. You remain apprehensive whether you will be able to face certain situation, whether you will be able to handle that challenging assignment, whether you will be able to answer the queries raised in the meeting, etc. In fact, there are many situations where a person can particularly feel nervous as listed below:

Can you make the water boil without heating?

Nervousness during interview is a common phenomena.

- Attending interviews (for appointments, promotions, etc.)
- Attending meetings.

- Speaking in public or a gathering.
- Participating in group discussions and debates.
- Solving examination papers in examination halls.
- Attending parties and social gatherings.
- Stage performance in instrumental music, singing, dancing, acting, compeering, etc.
- Taking responsibility of a challenging project or an assignment.
- Travelling alone for the first time in train, aircraft, bus, car, etc. for a long distance.
- Giving a performance of your skill in a social gathering.
- Delivering a formal speech to an audience from the stage.
- Appearing before a higher authority for discussions.

The way to come out of the wall of nervousness is to question yourself again and again as to what will happen even if you fail in your performance? Hundreds of persons are failing in various things. How does it matter? If you think that others will think bad about you or will make a low opinion about you, then let them feel so. You are also thinking low of certain persons. How is it mattering to them? Further, it is only our illusion that people are thinking so and so about us. Nobody has got so much time to think always about you. How much time do you devote for thinking and feeling about others, leaving your own works? You will find that this very questioning will erase your nervousness gradually.

One practical way to remove nervousness is that try to do those very things again and again which make you nervous. By thus exposing yourself to those very things which you are nervous of, your nervousness gets a direct jolt. You will find that this solution works like a wonder.

■■■

Freedom from Timidity

There are few people who show a cowardly behaviour in all their actions. Such people never take any initiative and show no drive to solve any problem. In any emergency and challenge, they will never come forward to take responsibility and lead others. They will be looking at others to take the lead and they will always remain behind and follow others like a sheep.

They will never like to take risks. **And it is a law that one who never takes a risk can never grow**. No doubt, there is also a possibility of failure or loss in a risk but there is also the possibility of success and gain. If you don't take any risk, may be, you will be safe from dangers but you will also be deprived of many new adventurous and joyous things which always remain in the womb of every risk.

A timid person can't relish the beauty and grace of the newness of life. He is always fearful and thinks of only the negative and the losing side of every new

Have trust in yourself.

182

thing. In an attempt to save himself from falling from the valley, he has to deprive himself of the joy of the mountain peak also. In life, peak and valley of the mountain go together. Either you accept both or leave both together. You can't take one part and leave the other part. That is where the trap is.

The way to come out of the cowardly behaviour is to realize first of all, this truth of life that whatever talent, capability and strength anybody is having in this world or anybody has ever had, you also have the same, inside you. **What others can do, you can do too. The ultimate potential of everybody is the same in this world**: No less, no more. The question is only of awakening this potential and working or labouring in that direction. Some people are able to awaken that potential by their efforts and therefore, appear successful and different from others. Once this confidence is developed that there is nothing which you can't do, provided you make efforts, then you will find that your feeling of cowardice is gradually vanishing.

The practical way to overcome timidity is to deliberately do those very things which you are afraid of. This puts a direct blow on timidity. Then one should also realize that you are not alone in any endeavour. God is always with you guiding you and helping you if you are open to Him. Once you take the initiative for a right cause and take the challenge and adventure in your hand, you will find that from so many fronts, you have started receiving help, resources and guidance and it will appear that the whole universe is supporting you.

While undertaking an adventure, you may always think that there may be a risk of danger and harm to you and you may get entrapped somewhere by vested interests even if you are doing a good thing. In this connection, **please remember that life is a gamble. Various dangers and uncertainities are inherent in life**. No matter what precautions you take, how much safe you play, still there is no guarantee that you will be hundred percent safe because most of the things are beyond your control. You have to be mentally prepared to face any eventuality in life. **So instead of fearing dangers, learn to enjoy them like a game.** Remember that every challenge and responsibility also has an inherent joy and a potential for growth hidden in it, in addition to the risk involved in it. Moreover, if you try to think deeply what can be the greatest risk in a thing, you will find that at the most, you can die which in any case has to happen, sooner or later. How does it matter whether you die today or tomorrow? **You can only buy time but you can't avoid death totally.** Moreover, it is better to die early while working for a good cause rather than leading a dead life for long. **The quality of life is more important than the quantity of life.**

■■■

Freedom from Negative Environment

We seldom realize that the environment we create around us or have around us has a tremendous effect on us. And it is all the more so when we are in the developing stage (i.e., have not spiritually developed fully). By creating or living in a positive and spiritualized environment, we keep our minds uplifted and full of positivity. The environment affects

Negative environment has a bad effect on mind.

not only in a grosser way (as we perceive it through our physical senses) but also in a subtle way through its effect on the state of mind to make it positive or negative.

There are various ways by which we can create a positive and uplifting environment around us.

1. **Music**: Music has a great power to influence the mind and mood than we normally realize. It can change the whole vibration of our environment. *Satwik* music which consists of devotional songs, chantings, *bhajans*, classical music, melodious songs of old movies, songs of nature, (e.g., chirping of birds, moving breeze, waterfall, river flowing, rainfall, shaking of tree leaves, etc.) is an excellent way to keep your mind uplifted.

2. **Colours**: Colours also have a very great impact on your mind. For example, blue colour gives a cooling effect to the mind. Green colour gives a balancing effect. White colour generates feelings of purity and spirituality. Red and yellow gives stimulating effects to a dull mind and fills it with enthusiasm and vitality. Black colour makes the mind dull, lazy and full of inertia and shouldn't be used. Keeping this in mind, choose the appropriate colours for your rooms, curtains, furniture, doors/windows and your clothes.

3. **Photos & Pictures**: What we see has a great effect on our minds and affects our psyche positively or negatively according to its nature. Instal photographs and pictures of enlightened and great persons, natural sceneries, spiritual/religious places and temples/churches/mosques/gurudwaras, etc. in your house and office. These have a very elevating influence on your mind.

   It may be noted that the effect of actual photographs is much more than handmade pictures because a photograph is said to possess the actual vibrational content of that person or place.

4. **Good company**: The people you normally remain with or interact has a tremendous effect on your mind. Human beings, especially in their developing stage have a psychological tendency to imitate or recall in their minds, activities of other people with whom they are associated. This is how they are affected. There is also an indirect effect of others on you which is the constant impact of their vibrations upon you. If they have good vibrations, you will be affected positively and if they have bad vibrations, you will be affected negatively.

   Hence, be cautious in choosing your company. Just have limited but good company whom you have tested properly. Don't try to associate closely with everyone.

5. Maintain cleanliness and neatness in your surroundings. If your place is dirty, it is not conducive to the peace and growth of your mind.

6. Keep temperature, humidity, noise level, pollution level, etc. in your environment under control by installing necessary devices since there is an optimum level of these parameters under which our body and mind can function best.

■■■

Freedom from Prejudice and Bias

A prejudiced and biased mind can't see the truth. Truth can only be seen by a person who has a totally open mind, not conditioned and prejudiced by anything.

Showing biased attitude is a sign of immaturity.

What is a biased mind? It means either you are against someone or you are in favour of someone. Now the person with whom you are against, you will see his everything, negatively and the person, you are in favour of, you will see his everything, positively. You will not be able to do objective examination by a biased mind.

Why mind becomes biased? There are many reasons. Firstly, if you are not a spiritually developed person, then you get easily influenced by the ideas, suggestions and beliefs of others which are continuously pumped in to your mind by your interaction with the outside world. These beliefs and principles become embedded in your subconscious mind and you start seeing and evaluating everything in terms of these beliefs and ideas and not in terms of reality.

Further, any person who hurts your ego, you become against him and you start seeing every activity of that person with the eye of hatred and negativity even if it is right. Similarly, any person, who pleases your ego, you start seeing every activity of his (even if it is wrong) with a positive bias. So in either case, you are not able to see the reality as it is. It is as if you are looking something with coloured spectacles on your eyes and not directly with the naked eyes.

Spirituality advises us that we should never get biased either in favour or against anything just from a limited examination of something or just by seeing one or two activities of a person. We should be able to examine a thing from a larger perspective, from an expanded vision so that we can see it in its totality taking all aspects into account. May be a person has two negative qualities but he may also have ten positive qualities which we are overlooking because of our bias with his negative qualities. Further, a person may be bad today but he may always change tomorrow and may be a different person in the future. A human being is not a rigid or a fixed phenomena. He is a flexible and open ended being liable to constant change. Scope for change is inbuilt in our hardware. So we should always keep this factor in our mind while making any opinion about someone and our assessment should take the total picture into account. This is also called the factual and objective assessment which is not biased or influenced by any limited and emotional factors.

A spiritual person is neither against someone nor in favour of somebody. He remains simply with the truth and facts. That is, sometimes he may be in agreement with you and sometimes, he may not (depending on the truth contained in your statement). He never goes by personal likes or dislikes in taking his decisions and in evaluating things.

■■■

Freedom from Ficklemindedness and Indecision

You may have observed many persons who are always fickleminded and not able to choose and decide a thing. They are very weak in taking decisions and always in a fix whether to do this or that. Sometimes, they feel that they

I am not able to decide which watch to buy.

should do this or select this thing but after a little while, they are confused and start thinking, "Oh! Let me do the other thing". Even if sometimes they finally select a thing (or are forced to do so), they keep on regretting and saying to themselves "Oh, It would have been better if I had selected the other thing". A fickleminded person remains in a very confused state of mind and sometimes can reach the limit of madness.

There are basically two reasons for a fickle and confused mind:

(i) **Weak mind:** A weak mind keeps on oscillating here and there by its very nature. It is not able to stabilize at one point. To strengthen your mind, the best thing is to practise concentration of the mind as much as possible.

(ii) **Ignorance of truth of life:** As I have explained elsewhere, everything in this world is dual in nature, i.e., everything in this world has got some plus points and some minus points. Now if you want to choose a thing which has all positive points and no negative points, it is impossible. Because of this inherent duality, no matter what thing or field of work, you choose for yourself, nothing can be termed perfect or having all the plus points in your favour. In everything, you will get some advantages and benefits but also a corresponding set of disadvantages and problems. When a fickleminded person sees the positive points of a thing, he gets attracted to it, but as soon as he sees the negative points of it, he gets confused. Then he looks towards some other thing which has got some other set of positive and negative points and again he gets confused because seeing the positive side, he wants to have the thing but at the same time, seeing the negative side, he wants to leave it.

The right approach is to realize this fundamental truth of life and not to do too much dissection and postmortem when deciding about a thing or a person. Just try to take a decision or choose an alternative after a normal search and inspection, and then try to find satisfaction from the same instead of constantly comparing its plus and minus points with other things or persons.

■■■

Freedom from Over-accumulation of Material Things

We, Indians, are particularly famous for collecting more and more things in our house over a span of time. That's why we find that when a person becomes old and requires the least quantity of things for his survival, he finds that he has the maximum amount of things around him and he becomes confused what to do with them.

Over accumulation of things creates a tremendous strain on our mind and leads to depletion of positive energy.

With the passage of time, the number of things increase so much in the house that they become unmanageable and a source of tension and anxiety rather than a source of enjoyment. We don't realize the tremendous strain which we unconsciously bear on our shoulders by accumulating unnecessary things in our house. This is because collection of more and more things is not simply a matter of availability of money with you but it creates many hurdles such as:

(i) More things mean more space is required to keep them.

(ii) More things mean more security arrangements for them.

(iii) More things mean more maintenance and more upkeep for those things.

Now let me tell you that I am not advocating that you should not buy any new thing for your house. Actually, if you see deeply, the root of the problem is not the purchase of new things but non-disposal of old things. We go on buying new things but we don't dispose off the old and useless things. This creates a mess at a certain point of time.

If you can maintain a proper cycle of purchase of new things and disposal of old things then you will be saved from the chaos and mess as I have explained above. I may also tell you one interesting thing in this respect from **Feng-shui** and **Vaastu** point of view that over congestion of things in a place leads to reduction of *Akasa* element which reduces the flow of cosmic energy in the house related to this element. This leads to the ill effect on our health and reduction of our vital energy. The more the empty space in our house, the more the *Akasa* element and the more is the flow of energy related to this element and this has a positive impact on our health and energy level.

The best way to regulate this as I often tell everyone around me, is to adopt the principle of *one in and one out*, that is, if you buy one new thing, dispose one old thing also. This will constantly maintain a balance. For disposing old things, there are various ways. Either donate them to the poor or sell them to a scrap shop or a needy person around you or dispose them in an exchange offer or throw them in a garbage bin, if a thing is totally useless.

■■■

Freedom from Intolerance & Impatience

It has been wisely quoted by a great man **"Strictness for self and liberality for others is real greatness"**. What it implies is that although you should be strict for yourself but you should be flexible and tolerant to the mistakes and shortcomings of others. In fact, the power of forgiving others for their mistakes and misdoings comes out from the power of tolerance only. Normally, we observe the

Tolerance is a precious virtue.

opposite in life. We start feeling irritated whenever we see the faults and defects in others and sometimes, start shouting and reprimanding others for their mistakes and behaviour.

We should realize that no human being is infallible. Everyone including ourself is liable to make many mistakes and wrongdoings in life. It is not something unusual and is rather the price we pay of being a human. We should take a more understanding and tolerant view of the faults and shortcomings of others. Instead of showing irritation and anger, we should be more compassionate towards the weaknesses and shortcomings of others and mistakes committed by them. In fact, instead of accusing, we should rather try to find out why a person is behaving in this way. What circumstances have brought him to this stage and what can we do to help him? We should contemplate as to how by making changes in our own behaviour and attitude, we can indirectly contribute to the reduction of imperfections in the environment and the people around us.

Power of tolerance and patience are an invaluable possession for one's spiritual development. They greatly strengthen our mind and will power. Try to practise these divine virtues at every step of your life. For example, develop tolerance for the harms done by others to you, for the harsh words spoken by others and for the insults done by others to you. Exercise patience when you have to wait somewhere either in a traffic jam or in a queue or while waiting for a person to meet. Develop patience while getting some work done without making a hurry, while waiting for the outcome and results of something. Show patience in listening to somebody not cutting his sentences in between. Show patience in talking to somebody, speaking slowly and assertively, making no hurry and jumping between the sentences.

You will be greatly astonished to find a great power and strength developing inside you by the exercise of these precious and divine qualities.

■■■

Positive and Negative Qualities/ Emotions at a glance

I am hereby giving a condensed list of various positive and negative qualities and emotions for your ready reference. This list will help you to find out at a glance as to what you should gradually try to eradicate from your being (i.e., the negative qualities and emotions) and what you should gradually try to inculcate in your life (i.e., the positive qualities and emotions).

Positive Qualities and Emotions

Adjustment & Adaptability	Understanding others
Compassion	Harmony
Concentration	Clarity of thoughts
Contentment	Willpower, Determination
Courage, Fearlessness, Boldness & Frankness	Straightforwardness
Democracy	Secularism
Detachment	Wisdom
Devotion (to work), dedication	Self-confidence
Egolessness	Positive thinking
Encouragement	Non-partisan attitude
Factual approach/objectivity	Fairness (nonfavouritism)
Faith, Trust	Self-satisfaction

Faithfulness, loyalty

Gentleness, Soft heartedness

Gratefulness, Thankfulness

Helpfulness, Benevolence

Honesty

Humbleness, Humility

Inspiration

Justice

Kindness, mercy

Liberality, Generosity

Moderation in everything

Non stealing

Non violence

Non-judgemental attitude

Patience

Planned & orderely thinking

Promptness

Punctuality

Respectfulness, Reverence

Selflessness

Silence

Sincerity

Smile, Cheerfulness

Surrender (to God)

Sympathy

Tolerance

Truthfulness

Display of responsibility

Optimism, Hopefulness

Joy

Creativity

Perseverance

Initiative

Foresight, Enthusiasm, zeal

Unbiased attitude

Balance & Stability of mind

Non-interference

Satwic lifestyle

Forgiveness

Purity

Naturalness

Simplicity

Amiability

Happiness, Beauty

Love

Self esteem (or self respect)

Non-critical attitude

Quick decision

Peace

Independent & Free nature

Calm and Cool mind

Assertiveness

Broadmindeness

Coolness/Calmness of mind

Negative Qualities and Emotions

Arrogance

Attachment

Attention on others

Blind belief, Superstition

Complaining, Blaming

Corruption

Criticism

Depression

Dictatorship

Disappointment

Dishonesty, Untruthfulness

Disrespect, Insult (to others)

Ego *Ahamkara*, Pride

Excitement

Fear

Flattering & pleasing others

Guilt

Haphazard thinking

Harassment, torture

Hatred

Hopelessness

Inferiority complex

Injustice

Insecurity

Irritation

Laziness

Lust or passion

Dependency

Non-adjustibility

Artificiality

Hostility & ill-will

Misunderstanding others

Insincerity

Judging attitude

Anger

Bias, Prejudice

Impatience

Confusion

Negative thinking

Eccentric behaviour

Worry

Phobia

Suppression, repression

Cruelty

Pessimism

Aggressiveness

Jealousy, Envy

Frustration

Neurosis

Favouritism, Nepotism

Abnormal behaviour

Hurry

Hypocrisy, Show off

Irresponsibility

Narrow-mindedness	Greed
Nervousness	Anxiety
Panic	Violence
Pity	Wavering (unstable) mind
Random & haphazard thinking	Overindulgence, Obsession
Resentment	Revenge
Restlessness	Helplessness
Sadness, Grief	Day dreaming
Sadness, grief, melancholy	
Sarcasm	*Rajasik & Tamsik* nature
Selfishness	Doubt, suspicion, mistrust
Spreading rumours & scandals	Carelessness
Superiority complex	Perversion
Talkativeness	Ficklemindedness

■■■

Few Quotes on Freedom

1. To know how to free oneself is nothing; the arduous thing is to know what to do with one's freedom.

   —*Andre Gide*

2. Man is born free and everywhere he is in chains.

   —*Rousseau*

3. No bad man is really free.

   —*Epictetus*

4. If a man doesn't enjoy solitude and aloneness, he can't relish freedom, for both are related.

   —*Arthur Schopenhauer*

5. Freedom can only be real if it is freedom and respect for those who think differently.

   —*Rosa Luxemburg*

6. What is freedom? It means not being a slave to any circumstances, to any restraint, to any chance, it means compelling fortune to surrender.

   —*Seneca the Yourgh*

7. There can be no real freedom without the freedom to fail.

   —*Eric Hoffer*

8. Those who deny freedom to others deserve it not for themselves.

   —*A. Lincoln*

9. As soon as one's freedom starts interfering in the freedom of others, freedom loses its dignity.

    —*Swami Sivananda*

10. Your desire for freedom should go along with respect for the freedom of others.

    —*Jawaharlal Nehru*

11. Freedom and responsibility go together. More the responsibility you are ready to take, more the freedom you deserve.

    —*Swami Rama*

12. Freedom is the root of democracy, the inspiration of art and culture, the dynamic force behind all progress. Its value springs from the very concept of human nature and it is important that it should penetrate all aspects of our educational activity.

    —*K. G. Saiyidain*

13. Men cannot be forced into freedom. They are unfree whenever the rules to which they have to conform compel them to conduct which they dislike and resent.

    —*Harold J. Laski*

14. If one uses his freedom wisely and properly, no limitations, restrictions or disciplines are required for such a person. Need for restrictions, prohibitions arises only when one misuses the freedom.

    —*Eric Hoffer*

15. Increase or decrease of freedom bestowed on a person depends on its use or misuse by him. Misuse of freedom (which harms others) results in curtailment of freedom while positive use of freedom (which benefits everyone) leads to increase in freedom.

    —*C.A.Bartol*

16. One hallmark of freedom is the whole hearted laughter.

—*Harry Ashmore*

17. Freedom is the most cherished desire of a human being. But it doesn't come free of cost. We have to pay a price for it by using it wisely and constructively for the benefit of all, failing which it is snatched from us.

—*Rabindranath Tagore*

18. Freedom means the capability to say 'yes' when yes is needed, to say 'no' when no is needed and sometimes to keep quiet when nothing is needed. When a person has all these three dimensions available, he is a free person.

—*Acharya Rajneesh*

Few Gems on freedom from the Great Master, 'Osho'

1. Freedom intrinsically means that you are capable of choosing both either right or wrong. If you are only free to choose what is right, it is not freedom.

2. Only freedom can be misused, slavery can't be misused. A slave has no choice to do right or wrong, good or bad. He is like animal on whom no responsibility can be thrown.

3. Freedom gives you the opportunity either to fall below the animals or to rise above the angels. It leaves both directions open to you.

4. Freedom is the supreme value. Nothing is higher than that. If a choice is given to me between Freedom and Love, I will choose freedom.

5. The moment you realize that you are only and fully responsible for your life, you are the most free man in the world.

6. Freedom is the criterion. Anything that gives you freedom is right and anything that destroys your freedom is wrong.

7. Only a slave can be imprisoned. A free man can't be imprisoned. He can live in the prison and yet be free.

8. An unconscious man can't be free. Freedom comes as a consequence of consciousness. An unconscious man exists like a machine, like a robot which is never free.

9. Freedom means having the courage to go into the unknown, not knowing where one is going, not knowing what is going to happen in the next moment.

10. Freedom means tremendous responsibility. You are on your own and alone.

■■■

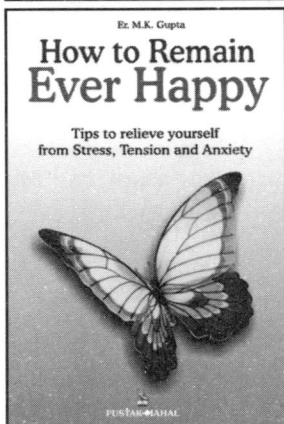

How to Remain Ever Happy

Er. M.K. Gupta

Tips to relieve yourself
from Stress, Tension and Anxiety

PUSTAK MAHAL

Everybody wishes to remain happy at all times, but very few discover true long-term happiness. Happiness, however, is a state of mind that can be attained at any time, provided we develop the right attitude towards all things in life.

This book contains 115 major guidelines, which include countless minor tips, that teach you how to cultivate the right habits and attitudes. Written in a stand-alone fashion, you could open the book at any page and read the specific guideline before you. As you imbibe and practise these teachings, you will notice your life being transformed, hour-by-hour and day-by-day.

To rephrase the opening lines in the book: *If you wait to be happy, you will wait forever. If you learn to be happy right now, you will be happy forever.* So why wait? Simply read this book and learn all the secrets of happiness.

Demy size • Pages: 156 • Price: Rs. 68/- • Postage: Rs. 15/-

Everybody falls prey to anger at some time or the other and says or does things that cause long-term damage. Once our anger has subsided, we realise the folly in losing our temper and severely regret our outburst and its harmful consequences. From seers and saints to common folk, people have spoken or written about how to control anger. But most approaches fail. This is solely because the physiology and psychology of anger have not been intimately understood.

How to Control Anger scientifically explores all the physical, mental, environmental and other causes of anger, seeking to eliminate the destructive emotion from its very roots. The book then spells out various short-term and long-term measures for readers to successfully conquer anger by taking into account the physiological and psychological causes.

Once you learn to control anger, your life will never be the same again. This book will allow you to become the master of your own destiny, rather than allow it to fall prey to fleeting moments of anger that leave permanent scars.

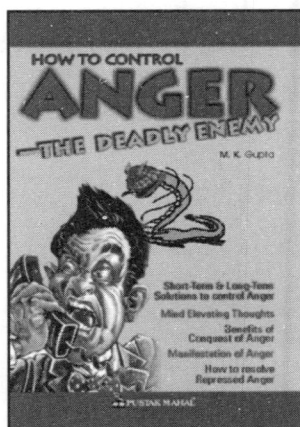

Demy size • Pages: 64 • Price: Rs. 60/- • Postage: Rs. 10/-

For millennia, spiritual seekers and scientific speakers have all stressed the importance of mind control in the pursuit of happiness and a stress-free existence. But the spiritualists missed out on the scientific aspects and the scientists ignored the spiritual side, with the result that very few were able to truly control their minds.

This book seeks to bridge that gap by helping readers understand both the spiritual and scientific aspects of mind control. It lets readers comprehend the true nature of the mind and how negative thoughts and stress are created by it. Spiritual and scientific techniques to control the mind and overcome stress are then revealed, which include meditation, yogasanas and hydrotherapy, among others. Once you learn to control your mind, peace and happiness come about as a natural consequence.

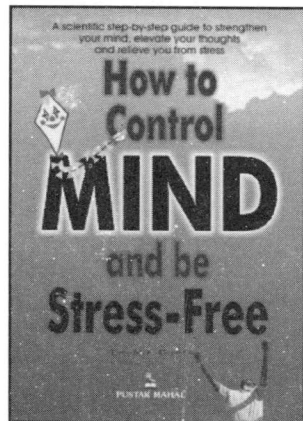

Demy Size • Pages: 136 • Price: Rs. 68/- • Postage: Rs. 15/-

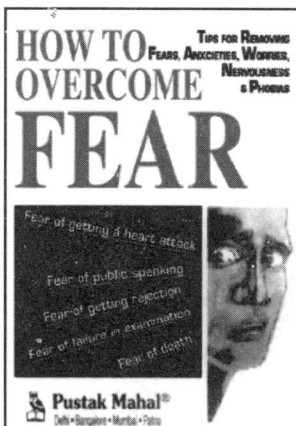

At some time or the other, all of us are beset by fears, most of them unfounded. Rational or irrational, these fears take hold of our minds, making lives miserable and bodies prone to disease and death. Indeed, the fear of death is one of the biggest and most widespread fears. In almost all cases, however, our fears are generated internally and have little basis in fact. Yet, all attempts to overcome it prove futile.

This book helps readers overcome their fears by understanding the various types of fears and their root causes. *How to Overcome Fear* then deals with the biggest fear of all: the fear of death. The author tells readers that there is another life after death, which is not the end of the world.

Once the fear of death is overcome, all other fears fall by the wayside and are much easier to control and conquer. By helping readers comprehend the physiology and psychology of fear and all the root causes, the book helps them overcome their fears forever.

Demy size • Pages: 80 • Price: Rs. 48/- • Postage: Rs. 10/-

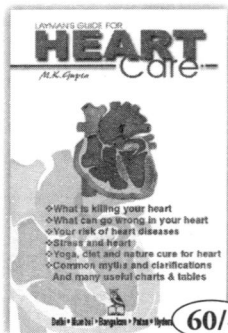
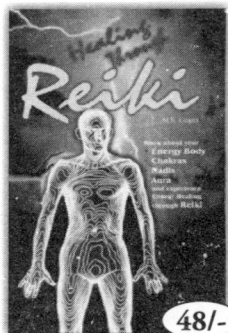
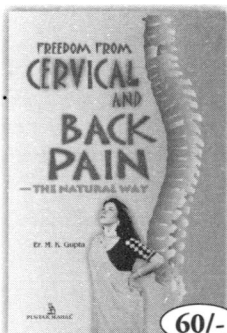
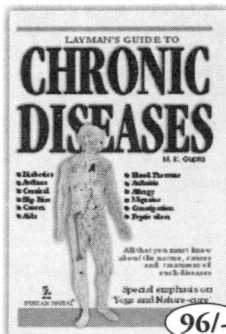

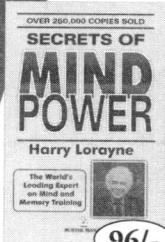

96/-

80/-

96/-

60/-

120/-

68/-

80/-

80/-

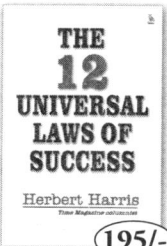

195/-

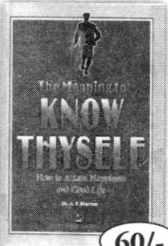

60/-

96/-

80/-

80/-

88/-

80/-

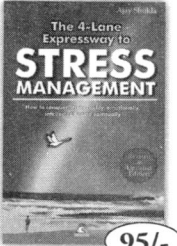

95/-

Postage: Rs. 15/- extra on each book